Recent Titles in Contributions in Legal Studies
Series Editor: Paul L. Murphy

The Network of Control: State Supreme Courts and State Security Statutes, 1920–1970
Carol E. Jenson

Drugs and Information Control: The Role of Men and Manipulation in the Control of Drug Trafficking
Jerald W. Cloyd

State Supreme Courts: Policymakers in the Federal System
Mary Cornelia Porter and G. Alan Tarr, editors

The Future of Our Liberties: Perspectives on the Bill of Rights
Stephen C. Halpern, editor

Tightening the Reins of Justice in America: A Comparative Analysis of the Criminal Jury Trial in England and the United States
Michael H. Graham

The Development of Law on the Rocky Mountain Frontier: Civil Law and Society, 1850–1912
Gordon Morris Bakken

Clients and Lawyers: Securing the Rights of Diabled Persons
Susan M. Olson

The New High Priests: Lawyers in Post-Civil War America
Gerald W. Gawalt, editor

The Little Rock Crisis: A Constitutional Interpretation
Tony Freyer

Nuclear Weapons and Law
Arthur Selwyn Miller and Martin Feinrider, editors

Native American Aliens: Disloyalty and the Renunciation of Citizenship by Japanese Americans during World War II
Donald E. Collins

Corwin's Constitution: Essays and Insights of Edward S. Corwin
Kenneth D. Crews, editor

The Role of State Supreme Courts in the New Judicial Federalism
Susan P. Fino

Church-State Relationships in America
Gerard V. Bradley

Rocky Mountain Constitution Making, 1850–1912
Gordon Morris Bakken

First Use of Nuclear Weapons: Under the Constitution, Who Decides?
Peter Raven-Hansen, editor

JUDICIAL SELECTION

The Cross-Evolution of French and American Practices

Mary L. Volcansek and
Jacqueline Lucienne Lafon

Contributions in Legal Studies, Number 40

GREENWOOD PRESS
New York • Westport, Connecticut • London

Library of Congress Cataloging-in-Publication Data

Volcansek, Mary L., 1948–
Judicial selection.

(Contributions in legal studies, ISSN 0147-1074 ;
no. 40)
Bibliography: p.
Includes index.
1. Judges—United States—Selection and appointment.
2. Political questions and judicial power—United States.
3. Judges—France—Selection and appointment.
4. Political questions and judicial power—France.
I. Lafon, Jacqueline Lucienne. II. Title. III. Series.
K2146.V65 1987 347.73′14 87-11890
347.30714
ISBN 0-313-26013-3 (lib. bdg. : alk. paper)

British Library Cataloguing in Publication Data is available.

Library of Congress Catalog Card Number: 87-11890
ISBN: 0-313-26013-3
ISSN: 0147-1074

First published in 1988

Greenwood Press, Inc.
88 Post Road West, Westport, Connecticut 06881

Printed in the United States of America

The paper used in this book complies with the Permanent Paper Standard issued by the National Information Standards Organization (Z39.48-1984).

10 9 8 7 6 5 4 3 2 1

For our parents,
Dick and Leota Matthews
Jean and Marguerite Lafon

Contents

JUDICIAL SELECTION

Chapter 1

Political Culture and Judicial Systems

Political cultures develop from the peculiar social, economic, and historical experiences of a nation. Cultural configurations offer perhaps the single most important explanations for why certain institutions thrive in one nation and languish in another. The judiciary of a nation, as any other governmental institution, is affected by the culture in which it is located. Innovations and experiments in judicial structures and judicial powers have been resilient in some cultures despite pervasive criticisms, whereas similar experiments have been short-lived in others. Implicit in the question of the role and power of the judiciary in a country's scheme of political power distribution is the issue of who names the judges. "Recruitment is perhaps the key link between a culture and its judiciary," according to Grossman and Sarat, because it encompasses "the means to reinforce old values and inculcate new ones through the socialization of decision-makers."[1] Lodging the authority to designate judges in the executive, the legislature, the people, or some combination thereof has a direct bearing on how judicial power will be exercised. This book considers the evolution of judicial organizations and judicial selection mechanisms in two distinct Western political cultures, French and American.

Debates on the best method for selecting judges are ongoing in legal, editorial, and academic circles. The controversy has tended to be characterized either by rhetoric or by empirical testing of the alleged failures and benefits of the various elective, appointive, and civil service systems currently in use in the West. The issues revolve around preferences for judges who are accountable to the public or who are independent. The philosophical and historical origins of the two positions tend to be ignored, as "whether judges should be independent or held accountable for the exercise of their powers is," according to Dubois, "a value laden question that empirical research is ill-equipped to resolve."[2] A consequence of this relatively prevalent attitude is that fundamental issues of judicial power, political power, and the judicial role are set aside. This book confronts the origins, both normative and political, that affected the evolution of the schemes now used in the United States and France. Further, our effort is a recognition that only through cross-cultural analysis can answers about law and politics that transcend a single nation-state be found[3] and that theory building about judicial institutions as political structures proceed.[4]

Judges, like members of other political elites, are crucial to the political process of allocating values for society. The parameters of their influence in this political realm vary in different institutional and cultural settings. Judges are, for example, generally recognized as policy-makers in the United States. Prerogatives of judges in other places, such as France, are much more limited and do not extend to invalidation of governmental and bureaucratic actions. Regardless of the precise sphere of power of judges in a given society, those who sit on the bench are important players in the schemes of political power and societal values. The selection of jurists, therefore, becomes an important variable in political equations.

The success of comparative inquiry largely depends on a conceptual framework that is capable of providing a common matrix into which political activity, events, and behavior can be placed. Recruitment of judges is the framework we have chosen, for, in its broadest sense, the term refers to all of the processes by which a judge arrives at his position. The term includes not only the formal process of selection, whether by election or by competitive examination, but also qualifications (formal and informal), availability of opportunities, and career ladders that lead to a judicial position. Seligman and his associates have broken the recruitment process into three phases: certification, selection, and role assignment. They explain:

> The first, certification, derives from a person's status in the structure of political opportunity, his opportunity costs and political socialization. The second phase, selection, involves the interaction between aspirants, candidates, sponsors and [the selecting body]. The final phase, role assignment, chooses the candidate and legitimizes his assumption of the office.[5]

This process may be envisioned as a funnel, in which individuals are progressively excluded from consideration as each stage further defines who is eligible. "In each phase, individuals are selected and rejected; some are winners, others are losers."[6] At various times certain ascriptive criteria (age, social status, race, religion, legitimacy of birth, or sex) have been formally established for judicial positions. In other eras, particularly during the latter half of this century, achievements, such as legal education, examination scores, and apprenticeships, have been emphasized. Nonetheless, ascriptive elements may continue to affect judicial recruitment covertly or indirectly. Shifts and changes in the certification and selection phases of judicial recruitment in both nations are the focus of this study.

Much attention in the United States has been placed on the effects of recruitment processes on the character of the bench.[7] More recently, scholarly research has attempted to determine if women and minorities follow different paths to the bench.[8] Interest in the characteristics of the judges who are selected is predicated on the assumption that the complex of background characteristics of any given judge will affect how that person will perform in office. Perceptions of the proper role of the judiciary and of particular policy preferences are assumed to be formed by the experiences that precede one's becoming a judge.

The formal mechanism for selecting judges has a direct effect on the nature of the judge who will serve. A consequence of this recognition has been that various modes of judicial selection have been tried in the Western world. Ideology is only one factor that affects the selection systems used. Social policies, such as increasing the number of women and minorities on the bench, political considerations, and practical realities of legal training and judicial temperament, may also influence the formal selection scheme used in a nation. The importance of a nation's political culture is critical for establishing priorities among these various potential objectives.

POLITICAL CULTURE

Almond and Verba defined political culture more than two decades ago as referring to "attitudes toward the political system and its various parts, and attitudes toward the role of the self in the system."[9] The concept was chosen to consider political phenomena because of its value in explaining the emergence and transformation of political systems. The notion of political culture has been recognized as "one of the most powerful themes of classical literature" but has not been viewed as a theory *per se*.[10] Rather, political culture "refers to a set of variables which may be used in the construction of theories,"[11] which is both a dependent and an independent variable for the explanation of political structures and institutions.[12] The concept of political culture has been frequently used and often contested over the twenty years since Almond and Verba first explored its heuristic capability. Despite frequent criticisms, among them the offensiveness "native" of stereotypes, there do exist national cultures. And the focus of the comparative researcher are those aspects of a national culture that are most salient to the research question.[13]

Dogan and Pelassy note the difficulty of speaking of a French or an American political culture.[14] We propose, in this volume, not to describe the two national cultures, but to rely on the concept to explain how and why structures for judicial recruitment developed and evolved in France and the United States over two centuries. The recruitment of jurists is the point where law and political culture intersect in a tangible fashion. Approaches to judicial recruitment evolve, if not parallel, at least in some tandem arrangement, with changes in a nation's political orientations. Evidence of the ongoing evolution of political cultures (and of the potential misperceptions of foreign analysts) lies in the determination of Almond and Verba in their original five-nation study to exclude France because "her democratic future [was] in doubt."[15] Democracy in France obviously survived and flourished, but the Gaullist regime and fragmented party system made a significant impact on the political orientations of the French policy and on the schemes used to name judges.

There are a number of studies of political culture in the United States and France, some impressionistic, some journalistic, and some rigorously empirical. At this point, however, we believe that only certain prominent features of each nation's political orientations are relevant. First, the United States has enjoyed a long period of essentially stable democracy, reflected in considerable institutional continuity. France, on the other hand, has experienced democratic instability that has resulted in seventeen constitutions since the Revolution of 1789. Second, through advances in communications and other technologies, both nations have become relatively homogenized. Yet the centralized structure of the French political system has, for long periods, thwarted regional diversity in political structures, whereas the American federal system has permitted, even encouraged, experimentation in governmental schemes, particularly with regard to the means of naming judges. These similarities and differences provide an overarching background for our consideration of judicial recruitment in France and the United States.

THE LOGIC OF COMPARISON

The age-old idea of philosophers that "knowledge of the self is gained through knowledge of others"[16] led us to the conclusion that a comparison of the development of the French and American methods for selecting judges might shed light on the desirability of various approaches to designating judges and might add some appreciation to the value and heritage of these methods. These two nations are particularly appropriate for consideration jointly, as the French system for naming judges, who form a *corps* akin to the civil service and are trained for their positions, has become the model for judicial organizations in most of the continental nations of Europe and many in Latin America. Indeed, "if imitation may be regarded as indication of approval," Henry Abraham asserts, "the popularity and acceptance of the French judicial system among the older as well as the newer states of the world represent such approval in the highest degree."[17] The U.S. judicial system, on the other hand, is derived from British traditions and yet represents, in many ways, a dramatic departure from that heritage. Aspects of the national court system of the United States have been emulated elsewhere, but other Western nations have not followed the American lead in naming jurists—in some states at least—through the electoral process. Interestingly, however, a form of election is also used in the Soviet Union and for some judgeships in Switzerland[18] and France.[19]

Through comparison of two major nation-states that share many common traditions (legal system is not one of them), we anticipated that additional dimensions and new insights on the merits of each mode of judicial selection would become more apparent. Comparison may well be the antidote for the danger of ethnocentrism,[20] which has been so typical of discussions of judicial selection. Indeed, few nations have been more chauvinistic in their assertions of the primacy of their systems than France and the United States. Yet the roots and experiences of the French and American governmental institutions share many common traits. Even though the French legal system would be classified as belonging to the Romano-Germanic family and the American system in the common law family,[21] the values and traditions of law and government underlying both are remarkably similar, as both share the Western tradition. That Western tradition is best captured in the notion of "the rule of law," which "will always be concerned with relations between authority and the individual."[22] It is the guarantee against arbitrary action by government and can be seen in both common and civil law countries in the commitment to constitutionalism, which makes law a bond between citizens rather than a source of political power.[23] This tradition can be seen in two historical facts: the continuous development of legal institutions since the eleventh or twelfth century and the perception of legal development as organic growth rather than as change. Indeed, as Harold Berman notes, "even the great national revolutions of the past . . . eventually made peace with the legal tradition they or some of their leaders had set out to destroy."[24] The roots of this legal tradition lie in the Roman Republic and the Roman Empire.[25]

The American and French revolutions occurred within less than two decades of each other. In both cases the pre-revolutionary schemes for designating judges under a monarchy were rejected. The British method of royal appointment was no longer followed in the United States because it had often meant a dependency of judges on the Crown and on the politics of the king. The French Revolution, on the other hand, resulted in an end to a system of venality, whereby judges had purchased their offices, because the system had permitted too much independence for judges and had fostered more than occasional forays by the judiciary into political life. Although each revolution initially occasioned a denial of the preceding system, each new government was lured from time to time by earlier arrangements, from nostalgia or perhaps familiarity.

As both the Americans and the French began to formulate new forms of government after their respective revolutions, the arguments about who should be judges and who should name them followed similar themes. Those drafting new constitutions were concerned about the quality of judges who might be recruited under various systems. Wealth or property ownership was considered a qualification, since people meeting this criterion would tend to be more conservative, more prone to protection of private property, and more insulated from potential corruption. There were fears that appointed judges might be too closely allied with the regime in power and would, therefore, be susceptible to political manipulation. Elections were seen as being consistent with republicanism and democracy, although there was a fear, on both sides of the Atlantic, that elected judges might be swayed by popular sentiments more than by legal precepts. Another concern regarding elected judges was whether their training and legal knowledge would be adequate. Indeed, during the brief experience of the French with the elective system, carpenters, doctors, and others untrained in law became jurists. An appointive system was seen as having greater quality control, although later complaints about such a system in the United States included one that judgeships became instruments of patronage and were filled by political hacks, rather than by competent legal minds. Another theme in discussions in France and the United States was the tenure of judges. Possibilities included life tenure, tenure limited to a specific term, and tenure until a certain age. A judge's term of office has implications for independence, for accountability, and for removability.

Those drafting the U.S. Constitution and various state constitutions in America and those experimenting with constitutional changes in France were also influenced by many of the same major writers and theorists of the period. In particular, because of his theory of separation of powers, Montesquieu was of major importance to both France and the United States. And there was some confusion in both countries when attempts were made to convert the concept of three independent and coordinate branches of government into practical reality. The notion of a judiciary that was totally independent was alien to both, such that independence of two branches was more likely to occur than was a separation of three powers. On other points Voltaire was also influential for French constitutional draftsmen, although he was not of any real importance in the United States. What seems to be most striking is that both Montesquieu and Voltaire had been profoundly influenced by their perceptions of limited monarchial constitutionalism in Britain. Yet the Americans of the same period, while embracing Montesquieu, could not conceive that his wise writings could be reflective of the British system from which they had so recently broken. Further, Jefferson and Paine were generally affected by both the French philosophers of the eighteenth century and their perceptions of the concrete consequences of the French Revolution. Adams and Hamilton, on the other hand, relied more on the English liberal tradition of John Locke.

Although the American Revolution occurred first, it seems to have had little influence on the later French Revolution. Perhaps this is because "the French Revolution was neither a sudden impulse, nor an accident," but rather, according to Aulard, "in conformity with the history of France, not in opposition to it."[26] It was a revolution to reform an existing nation, not a rebellion to establish a new one. The French Revolution, however, had profound implications for the United States. Events in France made the term democracy respectable and provided a theoretical context into which Americans of the early nineteenth century could place their own experiences and aspirations. The French Revolution had its own ideological bases, ones that would be borrowed and adapted by Americans.

Subsequent to the American Revolution in 1776 and the Constitution of 1789, changes on the political landscape and in political institutions came gradually. Dramatic breaks that occurred in the United States were often results of major events. Jacksonian democracy, the American Civil War, the industrial revolution, and the Great Depression all influenced and altered the institutions of government, including, at times, the judicial organization. Essentially, however, there is a continuity in the basic outlines of government in the United States for a period of 200 years.

Shifts in attitudes and political institutions in France have been sharp and frequent. There have been seventeen constitutions or governmental schemes in France since the end of the *Ancien Régime* in 1789. The governments that have been formed since that time have been republican, monarchial, and Bonapartist. Some of the breaks were so sharp that once even a new calendar was instituted to indicate the advent of a new era. At times the organization of the judiciary was affected by the shifts; sometimes a transition in government provided only a forum for reconsideration of the nature of judicial power and its place in the governmental scheme.

Even so, in France and the United States, the essential elements of judicial organization and expectations of the appropriate uses of judicial power were settled in the early nineteenth century. Both nations at that time established the structures and organizations that persist to the present day. Adaptations and modifications have occurred, but the basic outlines of structure and organization were determined in France during the era of Napoleon Bonaparte and in the United States during the period of Jacksonian democracy. Questions of how to select judges were also settled in coterminous periods in history. The French decided that judges of the ordinary courts were to be functionaries in government—a concept that has been developed and that characterizes judges in the Fifth Republic. Jacksonian democracy introduced the concept of electing judges in the American states, a practice that, although modified and "reformed," is still used for some level of court in more than thirty states.

This book considers the cross-evolution of the two systems, with the expectation that such a comparison will clarify how the two systems ultimately diverged so dramatically. Whereas political culture is proposed as the single most prominent factor affecting the cross-evolution, a three-stage recruitment process forms the means of comparison. Who is eligible, who is selected, and who legitimately assumes the office of judge? How has each culture shifted priorities for judicial offices, and what have been the implications of these changes?

Certain political and legal variations within France and the United States must be recognized, as these differences have limited the potential scope of this study. France is a unitary state, with all power derived from and exercised by the national government.

The United States, on the other hand, has a federal government, in which power is divided between the national government and the various states. These seemingly simple historical facts have significant implications for all issues of government, including judicial recruitment. As a consequence of a unitary form of government in France, all debates on judicial organization and judicial power have occurred at a national level, and all decisions have been for the nation as a whole. The federal principle in the United States has resulted in fifty-one separate, autonomous judicial systems, unified only by adherence to principles of the U.S. Constitution and supervised by the U.S. Supreme Court.

The national government of the United States was established in its current form by the Constitution of 1789. That document provided for a method of designating national judges that has not been formally altered in the ensuing 200 years. Most constitutions for the original thirteen states preceded the national constitution. These documents, and the constitutions of the additional thirty-seven states, have undergone multiple revisions and incarnations. The states have frequently reorganized their judiciaries in terms of powers, structures, and mechanisms for naming jurists. There are no national restraints on the variations that the states may adopt. Consequently, in the 1980s, there were five primary methods used for naming judges to state courts, and there are probably fifty or more variations on these basic schemes. Therefore, when we speak of judicial selection in the United States, with the exception of the debates of 1789 at the national level, we are speaking primarily of issues for state governments and state judiciaries. Yet events occurring at the national level have been inextricably linked to trends and attitudes toward state judiciaries. Even though a national judge in the United States has never been elected, the actions of national judges have often formed the backdrop against which state issues were performed.

An additional note on the courts included in this analysis is in order. At the national or federal level in the United States there are two types of courts, constitutional and legislative. The former are the courts that Congress may establish under Article III of the Constitution. All of these courts are staffed by judges who are nominated by the President and confirmed by the Senate and who serve in their offices for life on good behavior. These courts are the focus of our discussion. Legislative courts, on the other hand, are created by Congress to perform specialized functions, such as the Court of Military Appeals and the territorial courts (courts established for Puerto Rico, Guam, and the Virgin Islands). These courts are all created by Congress under its authority in Article I of the Constitution, and the criteria for selection and length of tenure are variable, depending on the purposes for which each was devised. Legislative courts are, therefore, beyond the scope of this discussion.

States may also have various courts with specialized or general functions. Some states have complex judicial organizations. For example, Texas has two courts of last resort (supreme court and court of criminal appeals) and at least five other tiers of courts, four of which have jurisdiction in the first instance. The jurisdictions of these courts may leave gaps in jurisdiction in some locations, but more likely they have conflicting and often overlapping authority.[27] Other states have adopted unified court structures, involving four tiers of courts only—minor trial courts, major trial courts, courts of appeal, and a court of last resort. Regardless of the judicial structure of a given state, the states retain sole authority to decide all questions of judicial qualifications, selection, and tenure. All of these courts are included in our explanation of how the American judicial selection systems have evolved to the present time. Complete description on a state-by-state basis borders on the impossible. Consequently only trends and major variations will receive primary attention.

The French judicial system is essentially divided into two main divisions, ordinary courts and administrative courts. The ordinary courts handle all normal civil and criminal cases and do not include the very specific commercial jurisdictions. The administrative courts were designed to handle disputes between citizens and administrative agencies of the government. These courts issued from Napoleon's administrative order established in 1799 to monitor possible administrative abuses. This system of courts was an answer to the French notion of separation of powers. Administrative courts, rather than the ordinary courts, serve as a restraint on executive or bureaucratic actions. Administrative courts have evolved since the Third Republic such that they now have the power to annul administrative actions, to order the payment of damages, and to check overextension of administrative authority. Judges on the administrative courts have a more specific character and are not included in this study. Only judges serving on ordinary tribunals are involved in the discussions of how judges are recruited. The Prosecution Department has traditionally been considered together with the bench. Although each serves a distinct purpose, the two have tended to be governed by the same requirements, and members have moved from the bench to prosecution and *vice versa*.

The next four chapters consider how the French and American judicial systems individually evolved from their pre-revolutionary schemes into their post-revolutionary forms. Then the changes in the United States that began during the era of Jacksonian democracy are charted, as are the imprints on the French judicial structure left by Napoleon and his successors. That this volume is written by two hands, one American and one French, is apparent, particularly in the perceptions that one side of the Atlantic had about what occurred on the opposite shore.

That political culture is a determining factor in the development of national judicial structures becomes progressively apparent. Indeed, "a court's power in a society . . . turns in large part on the belief systems of its elites and people."[28] This relationship, Danelski explains, can be traced through the myths and symbols that surround a court's legitimacy and authority. Courts, as political institutions, should be approached through a consideration of past and current belief systems.[29] Thus, that the national political cultures of France and the United States have nourished some approaches to judicial recruitment, but have repressed others, is the theme of this volume. Such can be demonstrated in each era of the past two centuries, but it is most graphically illustrated in the contemporary choices that each nation has made. Political culture, or "the set of beliefs, feelings and values that prevail in a nation at a given time,"[30] has led France and the United States to diverge completely in their approaches to judicial recruitment.

NOTES

1. Joel B. Grossman and Austin Sarat, "Political Culture and Judicial Research," 2 *Washington University Law Quarterly* (1971), p. 192.
2. Philip L. Dubois, *From Bench to Ballot: Judicial Elections and the*

Quest for Accountability (Austin: University of Texas Press, 1980), pp. 27-28.

3. Theodore L. Becker, *Comparative Judicial Politics* (Chicago: Rand McNally, 1970), p. 381.

4. Glendon Schubert and David J. Danelski, *Comparative Judicial Behavior* (New York: Oxford University Press, 1969), p. 18.

5. Lester G. Seligman, Michael R. King, Chong Lim Kim, and Roland E. Smith, *Patterns of Recruitment* (Chicago: Rand McNally, 1974), p. 14.

6. Ibid., p. 15.

7. See, for example, Herbert Jacob, "The Effect of Institutional Differences in the Recruitment Process: The Case of State Judges," 13 *Journal of Politics* (1964), p. 104, and Bradley Canon, "The Impact of Formal Selection Processes on Characteristics of Judges—Reconsidered," 13 *Law and Society Review* (1972), p. 570.

8. See, for example, Elliot E. Slotnick, "The Paths to the Federal Bench: Gender, Race and Judicial Recruitment," 67 *Judicature* (1984), p. 371; Sheldon Goldman, "Backgrounds, Attitudes, and Voting Behavior of Judges," 31 *Journal of Politics* (1969), p. 214; Joel Grossman, "Social Backgrounds and Judicial Decision-making," 79 *Harvard Law Review* (1966), p. 1551; and Susan J. Carbon, "Women in the Judiciary: An Introduction," 65 *Judicature* (1982), p. 285.

9. Gabriel A. Almond and Sidney Verba, *The Civic Culture: Political Attitudes and Democracy in Five Nations* (Princeton, N.J.: Princeton University Press, 1963), p. 13.

10. Gabriel A. Almond and Sidney Verba, *The Civic Culture Revisited* (Boston: Little, Brown & Co., 1980), p. 2.

11. Ibid., p. 26.

12. Ibid., p. 29.

13. Mattei Dogan and Dominique Pelassy, *How to Compare Nations: Strategies in Comparative Politics* (Chatham, N.J.: Chatham House Publishers, 1984), pp. 59-60.

14. Ibid., p. 59.

15. Almond and Verba, *The Civic Culture Revisited*, p. 22.

16. Dogan and Pelassy, p. 5.

17. Henry J. Abraham, *The Judicial Process* (New York: Oxford University Press, 1986), p. 267.

18. Henry W. Ehrmann, *Comparative Legal Cultures* (Englewood Cliffs: Prentice-Hall, Inc., 1976), p. 71.

19. Commercial jurisdictions inherited from the *Ancien Régime* have always marked an exception in the French judiciary as they are composed of elected judges chosen from among representatives of the different trades.

Jacqueline Lucienne Lafon, *Juges et consuls. A la recherche d'un statut dans la France d'Ancien Régime* (Paris: Economica, 1981).

20. Dogan and Pelassy, p. 9.

21. Ehrmann, p. 13.

22. *Ibid.*, p. 49.

23. *Ibid.*, p. 48.

24. Harold J. Berman, *Law and Revolution* (Cambridge, Mass.: Harvard University Press, 1983), p. 5.

25. The nature of the Western legal tradition may best be described in contrast to non-Western systems. See Laura Nader, ed., *Law in Culture and Society* (Chicago: Aldine Publishing Co., 1969).

26. A. Aulard, "The French Revolution and Napoleon," in *Modern France*, ed. Arthur Tilley (New York: Russell & Russell, 1967), p. 114.

27. Mary L. Volcansek, "Conventional Wisdom of Court Reform," in *Managing the State Courts: Text and Readings*, ed. Larry C. Berkson, Steven W. Hays, and Susan J. Carbon (St. Paul: West Publishing Co., 1977), p. 22.

28. David J. Danelski, "The People and the Court in Japan," in *Frontiers of Judicial Research*, ed. Joel B. Grossman and Joseph Tanenhaus (New York: John Wiley & Sons, 1969), pp. 45-46.

29. *Ibid.*, p. 45.

30. Dogan and Pelassy, p. 58.

Chapter 2

Appointing Judges in the United States

The first state constitutions were drafted in 1776 in conjunction with the Declaration of Independence. The national constitution, as it is known today, was not drafted until 1787. Before that date the states had acted as a loose confederation in which each state retained significant independence of action. The governing document under which this confederation operated was the Articles of Confederation, which had been drafted shortly after independence was proclaimed. These articles provided for a Congress of the several states, with meager powers, since exercise of important powers was contingent on consent of nine of the thirteen states and since there was no means of compelling the states to comply with determinations of the Congress. The Articles of Confederation made no provision for an executive office or a judiciary, except for ones that might be appointed by Congress for trials of piracy or crimes on the high seas. The basic inadequacies of the Confederation revolved around the inability of Congress to raise revenues or regulate commerce. Hence, a federal convention was called in 1787 to draft amendments to the Articles of Confederation, a convention that ultimately drafted the current U.S. Constitution.

In 1776 each of the original thirteen colonies began to operate autonomously under their newly drafted constitutions, although Massachusetts did not draft a constitution until 1780. The depth of commitment to familiar British traditions can be demonstrated during this period in the example of Rhode Island, which simply continued its original British charter from 1663. There were a number of reasons for the American Revolution; the dominant one, however, was not that the colonists objected to the British system of government, but rather, according to Margaret Banks, "because they liked it and were being deprived of some of its fundamental characteristics,"[1] such as taxation without representation and external control of their industry and commerce. Thus, that a variation of the British system of appointing judges was adopted is not surprising. All of the original state constitutions provided that judges were to be designated by the legislative body or by a combination of the governor and the legislative.

During the period between the revolution in 1776 and the drafting of the U.S. Constitution in 1787, two concepts of government dominated thought. Tensions between the two colored both constitutional debates and later issues in American politics, particularly in relation to the designation of judicial officers. The essential stress was between French intellectual notions of democracy and English liberalism, or, stated differently, between idealized agrarianism and pragmatic capitalism. English liberalism at the time of the revolution relied heavily on the writings of Locke, Harrington, and Adam Smith. Emphasis was on social, political, and economic individualism, without the interference of government. This ideology had a particular attraction to the middle class, a group that did not want to see its ambitions thwarted by excesses of government. French democracy, on the other hand, was an intellectual movement of fierce social idealism, which claimed Rousseau as its author. Liberty and equality were the main tenets of this school of thought. Translated into the American experience, English liberalism was favored by the middle-class mercantile interests, who sought protection for their property rights; French democracy, although more loosely defined, attracted the small property holders and agrarians.[2]

Ideologies offered abstract concepts, but there was little or no practical experience with republican or democratic forms of government in the eighteenth century. Consequently there was an inclination to emulate the governing norms that were familiar (i.e., that were British). The two competing approaches to the appropriate ends of government acted primarily to influence modifications of British governmental institutions that were required for adaptation to the United States. These concepts defined the basic parameters of discussions regarding selection and control of the bench. Limitations and possible variations on British modes were somewhat constrained during the revolutionary era for a number of reasons. Among the motivations for meager experimentation with judicial offices were the novelty of constitution writing and the absence of a defined legal profession with a dominant interest in the composition of the judiciary. Both British and colonial practices had included lay judges alongside and sometimes in superior position to judges with legal training. Thus the only preconceived notions of who ought to serve on the bench, for what term, by whom named, and by whom removed were formed by the British and colonial experiences.

BRITISH TRADITION

British influence in American life is particularly apparent in the means adopted for designating and retaining judicial officers. The British model and the abuses and corruption that flowed from it were well known to the American colonists. Indeed, the Declaration of Independence directly addressed the inequities resulting from the British judges: "He [the King] has made Judges dependent on his Will alone, for the tenure of their offices, and the amount and payment of their salaries." Whereas England had early announced that it was a nation founded on the rule of law, that ideal was not perceived as possible so long as the judges were dependent on the Crown.

The norm for designating jurists in England was appointment by the Crown, with tenure that was quite insecure, as it was, until 1761, at the pleasure of the Crown. As Vanderbilt explains,

> it was one thing to announce an ideal of the rule of law, however bravely, but it was quite another thing to achieve it. It was not for five centuries when it was enacted that a judge's term did not cease with the death of the king who appointed him, that the last vestige of judicial dependence on the crown was abolished.[3]

Abuses of judicial officers by the Crown had a lengthy history, dating at least to the reign of the Stuarts. James I, in 1616, asserted that because of his divine right to rule, judges were to consult him personally before making decisions. "Judges were the King's

Judges," Haynes explains, and "they were appointed by him and could be dismissed at his pleasure."[4] For example, when Sir Edward Coke persuaded his fellow judges not to meet with James I before issuing decisions, all of the judges were scolded and Coke was dismissed.[5]

A tradition of royal dominance of the judiciary can be traced through the reign of Charles I, who added exceptional pressures on his judiciary. Charles dissolved Parliament and was consequently without access to adequate funds. His solution was to demand forced loans from his judges. The Chief Justice of the King's Bench responded that the loans were illegal, an assertion that resulted in his prompt dismissal. Charles subsequently dismissed other judges for taking a position in opposition to him that proceedings could not be brought against members of Parliament for actions taken in the legislative body.[6]

Charles I was executed in 1649 and Cromwell became Lord Protector for life. Cromwell, too, exercised executive control of the bench, even though one of his grievances against Charles had been that the bench was being bribed. Yet the Lord Protector readily dismissed non-loyal judges in order to maintain his authority. Charles II, who replaced Cromwell, also promised that he would appoint judges for good behavior and would avoid the capriciousness of those who had preceded him. Yet he, too, removed judges whom he deemed too independent (i.e., who opposed the policies of the Crown).[7] In other words,

> Up to the time of the Revolution, although in general the judges held office during the King's good pleasure, the practice was by no means uniform; and the position of the Judges varied a good deal with the circumstances of the times; moreover the actual law concerning their status was not entirely clear.[8]

Subsequently the Revolution of 1688 appeared to settle that judges could not be dismissed at the whim of the Crown. Yet the Act of Settlement of 1701 (which did not take effect until 1714) again addressed the issues of compensation, tenure, and removal of judges. Dismissal, according to the Act of Settlement, could occur only on a vote of both houses of Parliament. Still the assumption remained that judges served only during the lifetime of the monarch who appointed them.

Finally, in 1761, just fifteen years before the American Declaration of Independence, a statute passed Parliament establishing that judges served for good behavior and were not dependent on the reign of the king who had appointed them.[9] Thus a semblance of judicial independence was given to the British judiciary. Undoubtedly, awareness of political manipulation of judges and justice by the Crown and the insecurity of tenure of jurists had an effect on the colonists in the United States and on the framers of both state and national constitutions. "The first royal judges and the American colonial judges were the king's creatures," Vanderbilt summarizes, and therefore "the need was realized for the immunity and independence of the judiciary."[10]

In the royal and proprietary colonies, with the exceptions of Connecticut and Rhode Island, judges were appointed by the royal governor, who used the offices for patronage. In fact, there is some evidence to suggest that the royal courts were actually small oligarchies. This is particularly important in that colonial courts not only exercised judicial duties, but also served many administrative functions. Chief among the courts' administrative powers were the assessment of local taxes and the supervision of spending for public projects. The courts also licensed innkeepers and paid bounties for wild game. Therefore, "because of the influence courts held over their lives the colonists were sensitive to the way in which they operated."[11]

More than one colony experienced violence because of the operation of the colonial court. For example, uprisings occurred in both North and South Carolina between 1767 and 1771. British tampering with the judiciary of the Massachusetts Bay Colony and later closing of the courts were likewise important events that fanned revolutionary fires.[12] Colonial judges had originally been governed by the same provisions of tenure that applied to jurists in England. However, when George III assumed the British throne in 1760, as part of his determination to regain prerogatives that his predecessors had ceded to Parliament, he limited the tenure of judges in the American colonies. Claiming that competent judges were difficult to locate, as learning in the colonies was so low, he made the tenure of colonial judges contingent on royal pleasure. He later established salaries for the judges of the superior court of Massachusetts and forbade the judges to receive any compensation from the colonial governments.[13]

These lessons of royal interference in the administration of justice were familiar to the constitution drafters of 1776. The frameworks of government adopted by the individual states during the Revolution are illustrative of how strong was the reaction against executive dominance of the judiciary. And by 1787, when the national constitution was proposed, a combination of the British tradition and the states' experiences affected thinking about the place of an independent judiciary in a republic.

EARLY STATE CONSTITUTIONS

The thirteen states drafted or adopted constitutions well in advance of the writing of a national constitution. One state continued under its royal charter, but eleven of the remaining had new constitutions in 1776. The Continental Congress passed a resolution on May 10, 1776, advising the colonies to devise governments that were independent from the British Crown. This resolution was, among other things, a means of pushing states that were hesitant about independence to commit themselves.[14]

Reaction against the British experience and an inclination toward French democratic notions seem to have influenced the thinking of those writing the first state constitutions. Indeed, writing of constitutions for republican or democratic governments was a novel experience; those drafting the state constitutions had little to guide them. Thomas Jefferson's reflections on the experience of writing the Virginia Constitution of 1776 summarize the difficulties of those confronting that task in his and other states: "This constitution was formed when we were new and inexperienced in the science of government. It was the first, too, which was formed in the whole United States. No wonder then that time and trial have discovered very capital defects in it."[15]

There were two prevailing themes in the deliberations of those writing constitutions in each of the new states: separation of powers within government and fear of the executive power of appointment. Both of these concerns had direct implications for the design of judiciaries, particularly in relation to the selection and tenure of judges. Many of the British constitutional struggles of the seventeenth century had been over the separation of the executive function from the legislative. Montesquieu, in his *Spirit of the Laws*, however, had not only proposed a separation of the legislative and the executive, but also contended that "there is no liberty, if the judiciary power be not separated from the legislative and the executive."[16] The British experience under the Stuarts' reign, in particular, reinforced the need to insulate courts from the control of any one person.

Yet the objective of separation within government in the minds of most Americans was to protect the legislature from encroachment by the magistry (executive). "Indeed, so rigid was the dichotomy in some American minds," says Wood, "that it was difficult to fit the judiciary into the scheme of government."[17] Most of the fear of abuse of the executive resulted from the power of appointment, as the power to dispense offices and titles in turn determined social and economic rank. The ability to give offices of profit was viewed as a means of creating social dominance. As a consequence, those writing the constitutions of 1776 were most intent on curtailing the power of the governors to appoint officials, particularly judges, without some legislative check. John Adams, in his *Thoughts on Government*, proposed that "judges, justices, and all other officers, civil and military, should be nominated and appointed by the governor with the advice and consent of council, unless you choose to have a government more popular; if you do, all officers, civil and military, may be chosen by joint ballot of both houses."[18] And indeed, his urgings were followed by those writing constitutions in 1776. Not one constitution provided for a gubernatorial power to appoint judges unilaterally; either the governor was totally deprived of the power or the power was shared with a council elected by the legislative bodies. In many cases (seven states) the power to appoint judges was placed in the hands of the legislature.

Judicial independence was a corollary to the concept of separation of powers. However, what precisely was meant by independence was not altogether clear to those writing the 1776 constitutions. Even in states in which judges were granted tenure for good behavior, there were other considerable dependences of the judges on the legislatures. Jefferson recognized this deficiency in the original Virginia Constitution. He noted that, although there was a recognition of the need for separation of the three functions of government, "no barrier was provided between these several powers." In fact, he explained, the judiciary was left dependent on the legislature for even its subsistence in office.[19] And, Wood asserts, judicial independence was further curtailed in that a vote in the assemblies was often sufficient to remove a judge from office.[20]

The new constitutions tended to be terse and lacking in details, for they were thought to be only temporary.[21] These documents also varied considerably in specifics regarding the judiciary, but they tended to follow two basic patterns for naming judges. Five states (Maryland, Massachusetts, New Hampshire, New York and Pennsylvania) provided that the governor could appoint judges with the advice and consent of the council. In most cases the council was a group of five to nine persons elected by the legislature, usually from its membership, to exercise the executive power in conjunction with the governor. Provisions of the New Hampshire Constitution of 1776 are typical of this arrangement:

> All judicial officers, the attorney-general, solicitor-general, all sheriffs, coroners, registers of probate, and all officers of the navy, general and field-officers of the militia, shall be nominated and appointed by the president and council; and every such nomination shall be made at least seven days prior to when such appointment shall take place, unless three of the Council agree thereto.[22]

The council described in the New Hampshire Constitution was also illustrative of that body's composition in other states:

> Annually, on the first meeting of the general court, two members of the senate and three from the house of representatives, shall be chosen by joint ballot of both houses as a Council, for advising the president in the executive part of government, whom the president for the time being, shall have full power and authority to convene from time to time.[23]

Other state constitutions (Connecticut, Delaware, Georgia, New Jersey, North Carolina, South Carolina, and Virginia) provided that jurists would be elected by the legislature. The 1776 constitution of North Carolina is typical in its provisions for naming judges:

"That the Assembly shall, by joint ballot of both houses, appoint Judges of the Supreme Court of Law and Equity, Judges of Admiralty, and Attorney-General, who shall be commissioned by the Governor."[24] Thus in no state was the governor or the voting population directly responsible for naming judges. These early constitutions may be viewed as attempts to preserve the power of the bench as separate from the executive, in which case the draftsmen were innovative. Some observers, such as James Dealey, contend that, on the contrary, the early state constitutions simply restated familiar features of colonial life, including a judicial system that was virtually unchanged. The only alteration was the transfer of appointment from the Crown to another body.[25] This view understates the importance of that transfer of appointive power, which moved the selection of judges to the hands of a representative body.

Most states gave judges constitutional tenure for good behavior, although some set upper age limits (sixty or seventy years of age). New Jersey provided for five- or seven-year terms, depending on the level of judgeship, and Pennsylvania had seven-year terms. In both instances the terms were subject to renewal. All states also specified some arrangement for removal of judges. For example, the Connecticut Constitution stated that the judges of the superior and supreme courts would hold their offices for good behavior "but may be removed by impeachment, and the governor shall also remove them on the address of two-thirds of the members of each house of the general assembly."[26] Some were more explicit about the grounds for removal and even took removal power away from the assembly, as in Maryland, where judges were "removable only for misbehaviour, on conviction in a Court of Law."[27] The legislative bodies maintained additional constraints over judges in that they were responsible for setting salaries and fees. This often meant, as stated in the North Carolina Constitution, that they were entitled to "adequate salaries during their continuance in office."[28] Thus the legislative bodies maintained direct control of the appointment process, either through a joint electoral ballot or through a council, and indirect control of the judiciary through determination of salaries and fees. Some question remains, therefore, about the true extent of independence for judges and of separation of powers in the first state constitutions.

By the 1780s, that these original schemes for dividing power in the state governments were impeding efficient administration of justice, in particular the disproportionate grant of power to the legislative bodies, was becoming obvious. Jefferson observed that

> all the powers of government, legislative, executive, and judiciary, result to the legislative body. The concentrating of these in the same hands is precisely the definition of despotic government. It will be no alleviation that these powers will be exercised by a plurality of hands, and not by a single one. 173 despots would surely be as oppressive as one. Let those who doubt it turn their eyes on the republic of Venice. . . . An *elective despotism* was not the government we fought for.[29]

Some greater attention to the independence of the judiciary was in evidence when Massachusetts, in 1780, finally drafted its first state constitution. The role and security of the judges were more clearly defined than in the other original constitutions:

> It is, therefore, not only the best policy, but for the security of the rights of the people, and of every citizen, that the judges of the supreme judicial court should have their offices as long as they behave themselves well, and that they should have honorable salaries ascertained and established by standing laws.[30]

Although what might constitute misbehavior remained unclear, at least remuneration was clearly provided as being "honorable" and secure.

Despite the legislative strictures placed on jurists in the post-revolutionary period, some judges insisted on acting with the greatest independence. The handling of the case of *Trevett v. Weeden* in Rhode Island in 1786 is a classic example of judges asserting their prerogative of independent decision. A crisis occurred over the use of paper money as legal tender for the payment of debts, what has been called the "political transubstantiation of paper into gold and silver."[31] The Rhode Island legislature passed a law making refusal to accept paper money an offense punishable by fine. A butcher named John Weeden refused to accept John Trevett's paper script in payment for meat and was thus charged and tried. He was represented by most able counsel, James M. Varnum, who argued forcefully that the legislative branch was capable of passing laws that were inconsistent with the constitution and that the judiciary had the power and the responsibility to judge those laws and to refuse to execute any law that was contrary to the constitution. Note should be taken that Rhode Island had not written a new constitution and was operating under its colonial charter of 1663, which makes Varnum's argument for judicial review even more novel. The court exercised judicial review and rejected the statute as an overextension of legislative power under the constitution.[32]

The offending judges were called before the Rhode Island legislature to defend their action. They asserted their independence from the legislature and their considered opinion that the law in question was unconstitutional. Although the assembly voted that the judicial explanation was not satisfactory, it did not take immediate action against the judges. However, when the terms of the judges involved in *Trevett v. Weeden* expired and the legislature considered their re-election, only one was returned for a subsequent term.[33] A similar confrontation occurred in North Carolina in 1787 when the highest court, in the case of *Bayard v. Singleton*, also ruled a legislative act to be in conflict with the state's constitution.[34]

The defects and difficulties resulting from the initial state constitutional provisions for separating the judiciary from the other branches of government, and thereby creating an independent body, were obvious to those attending the convention in Philadelphia, who would write a national constitution. At that convention Randolph commented that "our chief danger arises from the democratic parts of our constitutions." He continued that none of the original state constitutions had "provided sufficient checks against the democracy."[35] This sentiment was reflected in his Virginia Plan, which provided for a national court, appointed by the executive rather than by the legislature.

U.S. CONSTITUTION, 1787

Concepts of French democracy and English liberalism remained important in discussions surrounding the writing of a national constitution and in debates over ratification. The labels were changed, however, to democracy versus republicanism. Republicanism easily won out, partially owing to fears of mob rule, to interests in preserving property rights, and to acceptance of that which was most familiar. Experience with state constitutions, which gave greater emphasis to popular democracy through legislative dominance, was thought to have made the defects of such schemes apparent. Those who drafted the national constitution were pragmatists seeking to find a balance in government "between the economic interests of the major classes"[36] and were not inclined toward the type of egalitarianism that would make the rights of man superior to the rights of property. Following the teachings of great political theorists from Aristotle to Locke, they viewed property as the stable element in society and the masses without property as easy targets for demagoguery. Thus, those who met to draft the U.S. Constitution clearly "had no desire to place the reins of government in the hands of the common man."[37]

Apprehensions about granting power to the masses had been reinforced as western Massachusetts had approached a state of anarchy in January of 1787. The events, known collectively as Shays' Rebellion, were sufficient finally to tip the balance in favor of the English liberal tradition. That rebellion is of particular importance in discussing the role and place of the judiciary, in that the uprising was in no small measure an attack on the court system. The popular uprising by a group of ex-Revolutionary War soldiers (tacitly led by Daniel Shays) against the new state of Massachusetts was a protest against lawyers, courts, and the "idle rich." The legal system was a focus of their ire because it was lawyers and judges who sued debtors and who cast indigents into jail. In Springfield the riots were directly aimed at the courts, although the root causes of dissatisfaction were primarily economic. When the rebellion was finally suppressed, it became important for having "disclosed the danger" and thereby "helped to bring about a reaction, strengthen the hands of the conservatives, discredit extreme democratic tendencies, and aid the men that were seeking to give vigor to the Union."[38]

The republican position, that which prevailed, was perhaps best stated by James Madison in *Federalist* No. 10, when he defended the proposed constitution as a safeguard against the divisive influences of factions. The most important cleavages in a society, he noted, were between those who held property and those who did not, those who were creditors and those who were debtors.

> A pure democracy, by which I mean a society consisting of a small number of citizens, who assemble and administer the government in person, can admit of no cure for the mischiefs of faction. A common passion or interest will, in almost every case, be felt by a majority of the whole. . . . Hence it is that such democracies have ever been spectacles of turbulence and contention; have ever been found incompatible with personal security or the rights of property; and have in general been as short in their lives as they have been violent in their deaths. . . .
>
> A republic, by which I mean a government in which the scheme of representation takes place, opens a different prospect, and promises the cure for which we are seeking. . . . The two great points of difference between a democracy and a republic are: first, the delegation of the government, in the latter, to a small number of citizens, and greater sphere of country over which the latter may be extended.[39]

Those with property had a vested interest in the success of the government and therefore seemed to be the appropriate and wiser minority to rule the majority.[40]

That such a scheme was the outcome of the convention that met in Philadelphia in 1787 would not be surprising, if one accepts the finding of Charles Beard after his analysis of the economic interests of those attending the conference. "The overwhelming majority of members, at least five-sixths," he asserts, "were immediately, directly, and personally interested in the outcomes of their labors . . . and were to a greater or less extent economic beneficiaries from the adoption of the Constitution."[41] They represented the primary economic interests in the nation (public securities, speculative land, interest on borrowed money, mercantile, manufacturing, and shipping lines, and owners of slaves),[42] and "they knew through their personal experiences in economic affairs the precise results which the new government . . . was designed to attain."[43]

Beard's analysis has been questioned and largely discredited, as the economic complexities of 1787 defy a simple dichotomization of economic interests. Strict class lines cannot explain who supported and who opposed the new constitution. Whether the constitution is an economic document or not, there is a strong basis for the assertion that the constitution was not designed to promote or foster popular democracy. A number of provisions of the Constitution might be cited as evidence that the document was created to protect property and foster a republican approach to government by a minority.

The Constitutional Convention met in Philadelphia in May 1787 and continued its work through September. The Virginia delegation had taken the initiative in the first days of the convention and had drafted a proposed "correction" and "enlargement" of the Articles of Confederation. Edmund Randolph presented the proposal in outline form. The essence of the Virginia Plan was to create a strong, consolidated nation, with a national government capable of overcoming the defects in the Articles of Confederation. "These resolutions are important," according to Farrand, "because amended and expanded they were developed step by step until they finally became the constitution of the United States."[44] Resolution 9 addressed the judiciary:

> Resolved, That a national judiciary be established to consist of one or more supreme tribunals, and of inferior tribunals to be chosen by the national legislature, to hold their offices during good behavior; and to receive punctually at stated times fixed compensations for their services, in which no increase or dimunition shall be made so as to affect the person actually in office.[45]

The remainder of the resolution considered the jurisdiction of the national judiciary. However, the primary issue was the proposal for judges to be appointed or elected by the national legislature and to serve for good behavior. The debate that ensued on May 29, 1787, focused first on the appointment authority. In the debates two appointers were proposed: the legislature and the executive. Both James Wilson and James Madison spoke in opposition to appointment or election by the legislature because "experience showed the impropriety of such appointments by such numerous bodies."[46] Further, both felt that there existed a danger of "intrigue," "partiality," and "concealment" in such a process. Wilson argued for having the executive appoint all such officers, an idea not particularly palatable. Finally, a motion was introduced to strike "the appointment by the legislature" and leave that space blank, to be completed at a later time. That motion passed easily.[47]

Debates and discussions of the Virginia Plan continued over the next two weeks, with the greatest disagreements being over the basis of representation in the houses of the legislature. The divisions were largely between delegates from states that favored a strong national government and delegates from states that wanted to preserve greater power for the states. Contentions extended to questions of the courts only insofar as the states' rights advocates saw no need for national *inferior* courts, whose jurisdiction would either overlap or usurp that of the state courts. The need for a national *supreme* court was not an issue.

On June 13 the committee of the whole presented nineteen resolutions, which were essentially variations and adaptations of the Virginia Plan. Resolution 11 addressed a compromise on issues of dominant national courts and appointment to the national judiciary: "That a national Judiciary be established to consist of One supreme Tribunal; the Judges of which to be appointed by the second Branch of the National Legislature."[48] The remaining provisions of the original Virginia Plan regarding tenure and compensation were essentially unchanged. The provision for one national court had been proposed by Charles Pinckney and Roger Sherman. They had likewise recommended that judges be appointed by both houses of the national legislature but were overruled by the persuasive arguments of James Madison that the Senate was a "less numerous and more select body" and would, therefore, "be more competent judges and . . . was sufficiently numerous to justify such a confidence in them."[49]

Revision, but basic acceptance, of the critical elements of the Virginia Plan was beginning to appear to be a foregone conclusion, which was obviously a source of consternation for the smaller states, which feared representation in both legislative houses based on population. On June 14 William Paterson of New Jersey requested an adjournment for one day so that an alternative to the Virginia Plan could be completed for presentation.[50] The next day the New Jersey Plan, consisting of nine resolutions, in sharp contrast to the Virginia Plan, was presented. These resolutions were indeed amendments, not to the Virginia Plan, but to the Articles of Confederation. They addressed an extension of the power of the Congress, establishment of a plural executive, and a national court. Resolution 5 specifically dealt with the judiciary: "That a federal Judiciary be established, to consist of a supreme Tribunal the Judges of which to be appointed by the Executive, and to hold their offices during good behavior."[51] The jurisdiction of the national court was likewise much curtailed from that envisioned in the Virginia Plan. When a vote was taken between the two plans on June 19, 1787, a majority (seven states) favored the Virginia Plan.[52]

Consequently the convention returned to a report by the committee of the whole, which amended the Virginia Plan. The selection and tenure of the national judiciary were addressed in Resolution 11, which provided for selection of the judges by the Senate. Debates on the resolution continued intermittently in July, with Nathaniel Gorham of Massachusetts proposing that the jurists be appointed by the executive with the advice and consent of the Senate. His proposal found considerable support but was eventually defeated.[53] Thus the Committee on Detail concluded in its report of August 6 that "the Senate of the United States shall have power . . . to appoint . . . judges of the Supreme Court."[54] However, this was not the conclusion of the matter. In early September, David Brearley of New Jersey submitted a proposal to rewrite the section on appointment of judges to read as follows: "The President, by and with the advice and consent of the Senate, shall have power . . . to appoint . . . judges of the Supreme Court." The proposal was passed without dissent.[55]

What is remarkable about the debates, discussions, and conclusions of the Constitutional Convention is that there was no consideration given to popular election of judges. In fact, there was little support for allowing the legislature as a whole to elect judges because of the lack of competence and the excessive number of people involved in the House of Representatives. The primary issue was whether the Senate or the executive should have responsibility for naming national jurists. The recent reform in British practice, which was reflected in most state constitutions, was that judges should serve for good behavior. Tenure, therefore, was not debated. Compensation for judges, which could not be decreased, was also not a contentious issue. In short, there were not represented in the convention any arguments for French democratic notions. Largely, English liberal traditions, modified to better fit the American experience, were the only ideology considered in relation to the judicial system. Indeed, appropriate adaptations to representative government in America were the only relevant questions.

The result of the Constitutional Convention was the proposal of the Constitution, which addressed the national judiciary in two separate articles. Article II, section 2, provides that "he [the President] . . . shall nominate, and by and with the Advice and Consent of the Senate, shall appoint . . . Judges of the supreme Court." Article III states that

> the judicial Power of the United States, shall be vested in one supreme Court, and in such inferior Courts as the Congress may from time to time ordain and establish. The Judges, both of the supreme and inferior courts, shall hold their Offices during good Behavior, and shall at stated times, receive for their Services, a Compensation, which shall not be diminished during their continuance in office.

Section 2 of Article III describes the original jurisdiction of the Supreme Court and mechanisms for establishing appellate jurisdiction. Whereas there was little basic conflict in the convention over the establishment of a national judiciary and the appointment and tenure of those who would staff the national bench, there were dissenting voices raised in the ratification debates.

THE RATIFICATION DEBATES

The proposed constitution was sent to Congress, as constituted under the Articles of Confederation; Congress transmitted the document, without comment, to the states to either ratify or reject the new outline for a government. According to Kenyon, the circumstances of 1787 were optimal for accepting a new form of government and a new constitution. The difficulty was that a national constitution was not necessarily what many considered desirable. Kenyon further suggests that there was an inclination toward change among the American people because of their experience in working with their post-revolutionary constitutions for a decade. The defects and imperfections were apparent. And although there was a propensity for some to be doctrinaire in their thinking, many others were receptive to new political ideas and innovations. Thus there was a relatively fertile climate for approval of the new constitution.[56]

The new constitution was not enthusiastically embraced by all, despite the political tendencies to support. From the time the proposed constitution was made public, on September 17, 1787, until the ratification vote in New York in July 1788, there ensued a lively debate. The discussions have been characterized as "evidence of reason and riot, patriotism and propaganda," and as placing "sophisticated politics of the cloakroom" alongside the "crudest politics of the mob in the street."[57] There were essentially two (and only two) positions in the debate—ratify or reject. Pamphleteers, propagandists, and editorial writers assumed both positions, but neither the opposition nor the proponents had any real organization. The nationalists or pro-ratification advocates had at least an informal network of communication, but "nothing resembling a national organization had a hand in this fateful contest over the destiny of a nation."[58]

Opponents of the new constitution, the anti-federalists, differed in their criticisms of the document in many ways, but there were some underlying and consistent themes that their writings emphasized. First was the notion that the people were being hastily pushed to accept an untried, unpredictable, and novel system of government. The anti-federalists also underscored the legalistic argument that the convention that met in Philadelphia had no authority to draft a new constitution; it had exceeded its mandate. Another recurrent theme was the repudiation of the Revolution of 1776, as the new constitution was a drastic step in the direction of monarchy and aristocracy. And, not surprisingly, the final consistent complaint was that the new constitution stripped the states of much of their authority and would eventually result in the death of state power.[59]

What is noticeably absent from any of these general arguments is contention over national courts, except to the extent that such was implicit in allegations that the new government was not democratic and that all national institutions usurped the power of the states. There was dissension over the concept of a national judiciary, its proposed jurisdiction, implications for state judiciaries, and inferences of judicial review. Little was at issue, however, regarding the appointment and tenure of judges for the national courts. A perusal of the index of one collection of pamphlets produced in the constitutional debate is evidence of the concerns of the authors. There is a substantial number of entries under the title "judiciary," but the references are all to the power and jurisdiction of the proposed court system and to the encroachment of such a judiciary on the state court system.[60]

Not all of the federalists or anti-federalists ignored the issues of appointing national judges and giving them tenure for good behavior. The arguments against the proposed system, however, were not the same as would be encountered fifty years later. No one contended that judges should be elected. In fact, the anti-federalist tract *Brutus XVI*[61] even rejected the proposition that elections are the proper means of selecting judges:

> But it would be improper that the judicial should be elective, because their business requires that they should possess a degree of law knowledge, which is acquired only by a regular education, and besides it is fit that they should be placed, in a certain degree in an independent situation, that they may maintain firmness and steadiness in their decisions. As the people therefore ought not to elect the judges, they cannot be amenable to them immediately, some other mode of amenability must therefore be devised for these, as well as for all other officers which do not spring from the immediate choice of the people.[62]

Even so, *Brutus XV* rejected the notion that the British model of judicial appointments for terms of good behavior was appropriate for the national judiciary of the United States. Good behavior was required for British jurists because of their dependency on the Crown, which could, therefore, exert influence on the judges to increase its own power and prerogatives. But, Brutus suggests, "these reasons do not apply to this country," as there is no life tenure for the appointer and no passing of the appointing office to descendants. Thus, arguments for the British practice "lose a considerable part of their weight when applied to the state and condition of America."[63]

Alexander Hamilton replied to this argument in *Federalist* Nos. 77 and 78. With reference to the judiciary specifically, Hamilton said simply, "As to the mode of appointing the judges, this is the same as with that of appointing the officers of the Union in general . . . and nothing can be said here which would not be useless repetition."[64] This was an overstatement of fact, as earlier analysis of state constitutions attests. However, when Hamilton discussed the Presidential power to appoint, with the consent of the Senate, a number of officials, he argued that errors by either the President or the Senate would result in "opprobrium and disgrace." Were the President to make a bad nomination, he would singularly be responsible for his mistake; were the Senate to reject a good appointment, censure of the Senate would result. In other words, poor nominations and appointments would be precluded through fear of public outcry.[65]

Brutus did not accept potential "disgrace" of the executive or the Senate to be sufficient to ensure quality appointments to the bench. Instead, he attacked judges' total independence, even from removal for "errors or want of capacity."[66] Because the proposed constitution provided for removal of judges only for "treason, bribery, or high crimes and misdemeanors," Brutus suggested that another form of accountability for judges should be instituted: "I suppose the supreme judicial ought to be liable to be called to account, for any misconduct, by some body of men, who depend upon the people for their places; and so also should all other great officers in the State, who are not made amenable to some superior officers.[67]" He conceded that a court of impeachment, as provided by the Constitution, would serve that purpose, but he raised questions about the qualifications of such a tribunal to execute that trust.[68]

As noted above, Brutus rejected the criteria of tenure for good behavior. Hamilton replied in *Federalist* No. 78 with two basic arguments. First, he observed that this practice conformed to most of the newly written state constitutions and was "certainly one of the most valuable of the modern improvements in the practice of government."[69] He continued by explaining that an independent judiciary is a protection against the "despotism of a prince" and "the encroachments and oppressions of the representative body" because it "secures a steady, upright, and impartial administration of the laws."[70] Hamilton then explained that the legislative body could be called into account by the judiciary for passing a law that is not consistent with the Constitution. Therefore, the courts must be secure against the legislative body:

> If, then the courts of justice are to be considered as the bulwarks of a limited Constitution against legislative encroachments, this consideration will afford a strong argument for the permanent tenure of judicial offices,

since nothing will contribute so much as this to that independent spirit in the judges which must be essential to the faithful performance of so arduous a duty.[71]

Permanent tenure was defended as essential for jurists to pursue their duty of protecting the nation from oppression by the legislature.

The Federalist position, of course, won and the Constitution was ratified, first in New York in July of 1788 and finally in Rhode Island in May 1790. The debates over ratification demonstrate that, indeed, concepts of republicanism triumphed over notions of democracy. Even opponents of the proposed constitution did not suggest leaving the matter of selecting judges to the public. Independence of the judiciary was considered to be paramount as a check on the whims of the most populous branch of government, a position that did not merit argument. Rather, Brutus indicated mild concern over removal of judges and the ability of a court of impeachment as proposed to accomplish that task. In this, British practice prevailed, as did concepts of English liberalism.

REVOLUTION TO UNION

French intellectual concepts of democracy, to the extent that they had any direct influence in the constitutional development of the early United States, are seen in the early state constitutions. Liberty and equality were not fully embodied in these documents, but there was an effort to place the bulk of the power of appointment in the hands of popularly elected legislatures. Legislative dominance and a severely restricted executive were the most salient characteristics of the first state constitutions. Attempts were made, albeit halting and uncertain, to establish independent judiciaries. Even so, the experience of centuries of constitutional struggle in Britain between the powers of Parliament and those of the king had never included consideration of the courts as a separate power and function of government. The constitutional draftsmen in 1776 had difficulty conceiving of precisely how an independent court system might fit in the balance. The result was that they left judiciaries in most states largely dependent on the legislature. The legislatures appointed, either directly or through a council of their members who advised the governor, retained the prerogative to remove, and maintained control through the ability to set salaries and fees for the judges. The provision for tenure during good behavior had a slightly hollow ring in those states in which a judge could be removed for any reason, simply by a two-thirds vote of a bicameral legislature.

In some sense the first state constitutions were experiments in self-government that had elements of popular democracy at their foundations. These documents were likewise heirs of the British system and rejections of aspects of that tradition. Appointment of jurists was accepted as natural in the British tradition, but there was reluctance to permit the executive alone to make those appointments. The difficulties of insecure tenure for English and colonial judges provided a lesson for most of the colonies to assume that a judge's term of office should be secure.

A decade passed between the creation of the first state governments and the proposal for the national constitution. That time allowed most interested observers to note the defects and deficiencies of their own state documents, as well as those of the Articles of Confederation. Shays' Rebellion in Massachusetts was taken as a warning by many that democracy could easily degenerate into anarchy and become a threat to private property. By the time of the convention in Philadelphia, practical views of the validity of republicanism and English liberalism had taken sway. The convention aimed not at legislative or popular dominance, but rather at true separation of the functions of government, with appropriate checks on the exercise of each.

The first proposal for a national judiciary in the Virginia Plan simply replicated that adopted in most of the states—election by the legislature, with tenure for good behavior. Only the mild New Jersey Plan proposed a national court for which judges would be appointed by the President. Throughout the ensuing debates at the convention there was an apparent consensus that the judiciary should be appointed by the upper house of the legislature. That view was not altered until the closing days of the convention, when there was a proposal, passed unanimously, for the executive to appoint, with the advice and consent of the Senate. That tenure for judges should be for life or for good behavior, with a provision for impeachment, was not a contested issue. Even in the ratification debates that followed the public proposal of the new constitution there was little discussion or dissension over the appointment or tenure of national judges.

A number of factors combined to make issues of the judicial power of minimal importance to eighteenth-century draftsmen in comparison to finding a balance between the executive and the legislature. This is not to suggest that American statesmen were, in the words of Lawrence Friedman, "naive," for as he explained, "they knew that it mattered what judges believed and who they were."[72] Rather, lawyers and judges were not yet an organized and homogenous profession of which specific criteria and qualifications could be required. The lines differentiating jurists, lawyers, and laypersons were not yet clear. The tradition of lay involvement in the judiciary had ancient roots and had been a typical aspect of English and colonial courts.[73] Non-lawyers served at the base and at the apex of judicial systems in post-revolutionary New Jersey and New York. These lay jurists were typically politicians who represented the upper strata of society.[74] A result was that in New York a small number of landed families dominated the judiciary and upheld the interests of landlords in disputes over oppressive leases.[75]

Civil litigation was not the norm for settling disputes until at least the 1790s. Rather, church and town meetings served that function for most of the population. However, as commerce increased and more religious diversity emerged, reliance on judicial structures became progressively more accepted.[76] When people began to rely on civil courts to resolve their conflicts, then interest in and criticism of structures and staffing of courts emerged as political issues. Much of the subsequent anti-court movement resulted from allegations that the courts, whether lawyers or laypersons were presiding, were biased on class grounds.[77]

Until the close of the eighteenth century the legal profession had not coalesced into an organization that could be charged with political, economic, or class interests. Indeed, as Gerard Gawalt notes, in 1765 there were fewer than fifty trained lawyers in the colony of Massachusetts, although the population numbered almost one-quarter million persons.[78] The post-revolutionary period witnessed the growth of economic and political power for lawyers. Law even came to dominate religion as the course of study at Harvard College. From 1789 to 1801 the overwhelming majority of those elected to Congress from Massachusetts were lawyers. As the legal profession began to aggrandize power, there arose an opposition to it and to its ancillaries, the courts. Bar associations began to limit their ranks by establishing criteria for the practice of law and to guarantee their economic security by creating minimum free structures.[79] The bench and the bar became hostages of an economic class, which was then in a position to wield political power.

The nineteenth century brought a new set of concerns about courts—who controls them and what powers might they exercise. The early constitutional draftsmen could not have anticipated the importance that judges would attain in the popular mind when litigiousness increased or in the scheme of political power as courts evolved into overtly partisan bodies. Thus, within fewer than four decades, the issues of selecting and removing judges would reemerge in quite different guises, tied to quite distinctive issues. Nonetheless the themes of French democracy and English liberalism persisted as the main lines of thought about the judiciary.

NOTES

1. Margaret A. Banks, "Attitudes in the Philadelphia Convention Towards the British System of Government," 10 *American Journal of Legal History* (January 1966), p. 15.

2. Vernon Louis Parrington, *Main Currents in American Thought*, vol. I (New York: Harcourt, Brace, & World, 1927), pp. 271-79. Parrington uses the term French romanticism, which would be a misnomer before the nineteenth century.

3. Arthur F. Vanderbilt, "Judges and Jurors: Their Functions, Qualifications and Selection," 36 *Boston University Law Review* (1956), p. 14.

4. Evan Haynes, *The Selection and Tenure of Judges* (Littleton, Colo.: Fred B. Rothman & Co., 1944), p. 54.

5. Ibid., p. 58.

6. Ibid., p. 59.

7. Ibid., p. 72.

8. Ibid., p. 76.

9. Ibid., p. 79.

10. Vanderbilt, p. 19.

11. Richard E. Ellis, *The Jeffersonian Crisis: Courts and Politics in the Young Republic* (New York: Oxford University Press, 1971), p. 6.

12. Ibid., pp. 6-7.

13. William S. Carpenter, *Judicial Tenure in the United States* (New Haven, Conn.: Yale University Press, 1918), pp. 2-3.

14. Gordon S. Wood, *The Creation of the American Republic, 1776-1787* (Chapel Hill: University of North Carolina Press, 1969), pp. 131-32.

15. Merrill D. Peterson, ed., *The Portable Thomas Jefferson* (Harmondsworth: Penguin Press, 1977), p. 162.

16. Baron de Montesquieu, *The Spirit of the Laws*, trans. Thomas Nugent (New York: Hafner Publishing Co., 1949), p. 152.

17. Wood, p. 159.

18. John Adams, *The Political Writings of John Adams*, ed. George A. Peek, Jr. (New York: Liberal Arts Press, 1954), p. 90.

19. Peterson, p. 165.

20. Wood, p. 16.

21. James Q. Dealey, *The Growth of American State Constitutions* (New York: Da Capo Press, 1972), p. 39.

22. Perley Poore Ben, *The Federal and State Constitutions, Colonial Charters, and Other Organic Laws of the United States* (New York: Burt Franklin, 1877), pp. 1288-89.

23. Ibid., p. 1289.

24. Ibid., p. 1412.

25. Dealey, p. 38.

26. Ben, p. 263.

27. Ibid., p. 826.

28. Ibid., p. 1413.

29. Peterson, p. 164.

30. Ben, p. 960.

31. Andrew Cunningham McLaughlin, *The Confederation and the Constitution: 1783-1789)* (New York: Harper & Brothers, 1905), p. 149.

32. Ibid., pp. 151-53.

33. Ibid., p. 153.

34. Carpenter, p. 19.

35. Max Farrand, *The Framing of Constitution of the United States* (New Haven, Conn.: Yale University Press, 1913), p. 68.

36. Parrington, vol. I, p. 286.

37. Banks, p. 19.

38. McLaughlin, p. 166.

39. *Federalist*, No. 10 (New York: Modern Library), pp. 58-59.

40. Parrington, vol. I, p. 286.

41. Charles A. Beard, *An Economic Interpretation of the Constitution of the United States* (New York: The Free Press, 1935), p. 149.

42. Ibid., pp. 149-51.

43. Ibid., p. 151.

44. Farrand, p. 68.
45. Arthur Taylor Prescott, *Drafting the Federal Constitution* (Westport, Conn.: Greenwood Press, 1968), p. 659.
46. Ibid., p. 659.
47. Ibid., pp. 659-60.
48. Clinton Rossiter, *1787: The Grand Convention* (New York: Macmillan Co., 1966), p. 364.
49. Prescott, pp. 660-61.
50. Farrand, p. 84.
51. Rossiter, p. 368.
52. Farrand, p. 89.
53. Prescott, pp. 661-69.
54. Rossiter, p. 372.
55. Prescott, p. 671.
56. Cecelia M. Kenyon, ed., *The Anti-Federalists* (Indianapolis: Bobbs-Merrill Co., 1966), pp. xxxiii-xxxiv.
57. Ibid., p. xxiii.
58. Rossiter, p. 277.
59. Ibid., pp. 283-84.
60. See, for example, Paul Leicester Ford, *Pamphlets on the Constitution of the United States* (New York: Da Capo Press, 1968), p. 446.
61. "Brutus" is generally believed to have been the pseudonym for Robert Yates, but there is some controversy over that attribution. See Herbert J. Storing, ed., *The Anti-Federalists* (Chicago: University of Chicago Press, 1985), p. 103.
62. Ibid., p. 188.
63. Ibid., p. 184.
64. *Federalist*, No. 78, p. 503.
65. *Federalist*, No. 77, pp. 498-99.
66. Storing, p. 184.
67. Ibid., p. 188.
68. Ibid.
69. *Federalist*, No. 78, p. 503.
70. Ibid.
71. Ibid., p. 508.
72. Lawrence M. Friedman, *A History of American Law* (New York: Simon & Schuster, 1973), p. 109.
73. John P. Dawson, *A History of Lay Judges* (Cambridge, Mass.: Harvard University Press, 1960), pp. 287-91.
74. Friedman, pp. 109-10.
75. Patrick Winston Dunn, "Judicial Selection in the States," 4 *Hofstra Law Review* (1976), p. 278.

76. William E. Nelson, *Dispute and Conflict Resolution in Plymouth County, Massachusetts, 1725-1825* (Chapel Hill: University of North Carolina Press, 1981), pp. 131-32.

77. Friedman, p. 110.

78. Gerard W. Gawalt, *The Promise of Power: The Emergence of the Legal Profession in Massachusetts, 1760-1840* (Westport, Conn.: Greenwood Press, 1979), p. 3.

79. Ibid., pp. 81-91.

Chapter 3

Designating Judges in France: Monarchy and Revolution

For more than 200 years France practiced the system of venality, or sale of office, to designate judges. Writings of the political theorists and critics during the eighteenth century, together with the Revolution of 1789 and the decisions of the National Assembly, resulted in a total restructuring of the system. Part of the new judicial organization was an experiment, although quite brief, with electing judges.

ANCIEN RÉGIME

The institutions of the French monarchy developed substantially from the sixteenth to the eighteenth century. Institutional evolution during the centuries of royal rule was not necessarily in the direction of organizational simplification. Rather, by the end of the *Ancien Régime* the judicial organization was extremely complex. There were various categories of jurisdictions, but none encroached upon the adage, "*Toute justice émane du Roi*," or, the king alone has the power to dispense justice. The king was sovereign, and matters of justice were attributes of his sovereignty. The monarch could administer justice directly through his *lettres de cachet*.[1] This he could do without any control or supervision. Ordinarily, however, the monarch administered justice by sitting in his council or by delegating power to the royal jurisdictions or to the lords.

All judges, whether they belonged to the royal jurisdictions or to the seigneurial jurisdictions, had one common characteristic: they purchased their offices.[2] This was the accepted system of venality.[3] The principle of venality was recognized by the king of France in 1522 and completed by the principle of hereditary transmission in 1604.[4] Hence the judicial office appeared as a public function, which was a simple merchandise, the object of private property. To be precise, the word "office" encompassed the title that could only be obtained from the king. The financial value (*la finance*) that was bought represented the right to be presented to the king by the actual owner or his heirs in order to obtain the title, bestowed in "letters of provision." The venality of offices lasted until the French Revolution. The system of venality and the theories that were developed in the years preceding the Revolution must be analyzed to understand the evolution of the French system for designating jurists.

The entire judicial system was based on the purchase of offices. Therefore, a first logical question relates to consideration of the different judicial offices that were available for purchase. In such a context, did the judges benefit from their position (*statut*)? And did they have the opportunity for a real career, or was such an ambition inconceivable?

There were judicial offices at all prices, depending simply on the importance of the jurisdiction. For example, the office of a judge in the seigneurial court of Villemonteix in the province of La Marche was sold for 1,200 pounds in 1754,[5] whereas the office of a counsellor in the Parliament of Paris was worth 40,000 pounds the same year.[6] The office of *président à mortier* in the same parliament was not even comparable, with a price of more than 500,000 pounds. Regardless of the price, the office represented an important part of the patrimony or estate of the judge. A jurist often had to borrow the money necessary to buy an office and he could likewise mortgage it.

Some have observed that the prices of judicial offices were not very stable during the eighteenth century. The offices in the lower jurisdictions consistently tended to be less expensive. For example, the office of the seigneurial judge in Magnat in La Marche was valued at 400 pounds in 1730, but only 300 pounds in 1748.[7] The office of counsellor in the *présidial* (a royal jurisdiction) in Angers was worth 36,000 pounds in 1713 but was sold for a mere 3,000 pounds in 1760.[8]

Sometimes not all the offices in a court were taken, and consequently there were too few judges to make timely decisions. There seem to be two closely linked explanations for this situation: the profits of the office represented only a meager one percent of the capital invested, which was clearly insufficient, and as a result, the offices became largely discredited. At the end of the *Ancien Régime* there was a crisis, for in several *cahiers de doléances*[9] of 1789 suggestions were proposed to the king for the purpose of rehabilitating judicial positions.

The same general trend can be observed in the prices of the offices in the courts of parliaments, although that evolution is more complicated. In the Parliament of Paris the office of counsellor fell from 100,000 pounds in 1715 to 40,000 pounds in 1732 and rose back to 50,000 pounds in 1771. That price remained constant until the Revolution. There were multiple causes for this phenomenon—the feeble revenues, the obligation to belong to ancient nobility, and the risk of being sanctioned by the king in case of political opposition. Nonetheless these offices still found candidates ready to purchase them because of the honor, dignity, and symbolism of power and authority.[10] Having to buy the office of judge was not in itself an obstacle; moreover, it must be noted that one person could accumulate several offices. This was one way to compensate for the insufficient income resulting from a single position. The principle of multiple office-holding was criticized for centuries before being confronted during the eighteenth century.[11]

Judges at this time did have a *statut*. Although the term *statut* is a little precocious for the eighteenth century, it can be used because conditions were required to exercise the function of judge, a remuneration was established, and guarantees were given. A person wishing to become a judge not only had to find a vacant office that he could afford and purchase it, but he also had to meet certain additional conditions. Stipulations were more severe for magistrates of the courts of parliament. The candidate must be a legitimate son and a Catholic.[12] He must be twenty-five years of age to qualify for the office of counsellor and age forty, with ten years of experience, if he sought the seat of a *président à mortier*. He could not have any parent or near cousin among his future colleagues. If these conditions had been strictly respected, recruiting a purchaser for offices might have been difficult. Magistrates wanted to choose their peers from among the nobility and, more precisely, nobility by the robe, as opposed to nobility by the sword.[13] Such an attitude limited the pool of eligible candidates. This is why many letters of exemption were granted in the second half of the eighteenth century. For example, some candidate-counsellors were admitted at age seventeen, without reference to family connections.[14]

A candidate would pay his respects to each magistrate in the court to which he aspired in a visit. Candidates hoped to make good impressions, and thereby to win votes. While candidates were making the rounds of all magistrates, the head of the Prosecution Department would investigate the candidate's life and morality. Four witnesses would be called to testify, among them the parish priest.[15] Because candidates had usually just completed their law degrees, they were required to take an examination directed by the first president of the court, in the presence of the entire court. This was an ancient tradition that eventually faded into insignificance.[16] At the conclusion of these formalities and on a favorable vote, the candidate would be accepted as magistrate and given the oath of office.[17] Clearly most of these requirements were designed to co-opt novice magistrates.

Judges' remuneration consisted of wages, spices, and, in some cases, certain privileges. The wages were stipends paid by the king, which were supposed to represent interest on the judge's capital invested in the office. These wages varied according to the number of days a judge worked. For example, a counsellor in the Parliament of Paris, de Bragelongue, was sick a substantial portion of 1755 and was paid only 19 pounds, whereas the year before he was paid 362 pounds, even though the parliament had been exiled for eight months of the year.[18] In general, the wages were low and often irregularly paid. The same comment could be made regarding the pay of judges in lower royal jurisdictions. The *lieutenant général* in the *bailliage* of Riom received 300 pounds in 1742. Only very high magistrates (first president, head of the Prosecution Department, and *présidents à mortier* in the parliaments) were paid significant wages, but their expenses were also considerable.[19]

The judges, therefore, demanded spices to compensate for their paltry stipends. Primarily, the spices were sweets that successful litigants would offer to the judges. Progressively these gifts were converted into sums of money and, in the fifteenth century, became obligatory. One justification for this practice was that the spices were compensation for what the judge did outside his courtroom. The sum of the spices was divided among the judges on a court in proportion to the number of cases each decided. Such a use of spices fell into disrepute by the end of the *Ancien Régime* because the litigants resented having to "pay for justice." Additionally, the practice was simply awkward and did not appreciably increase the magistrate's income. Indeed, the counsellor Bragelongue received only between 200 and 400 pounds per year in the 1750s.[20] The final element of a judge's income was not money *per se*, but savings, such as tax exemptions.[21] The conclusion is obvious—judges could not earn a comfortable living. Family fortune and personal revenues were essential.[22] However, even though a judge's financial situation might not have been satisfactory, he did at least have solid guarantees of his tenure in office.

Judicial tenure resulted from the principle of irremovability of judges, an axiom first affirmed by King Louis XI in 1467. This principle applied to all judges, those belonging to the bench, as well as those of the prosecution. This meant that under no circumstances could the king remove a magistrate whom he had nominated. The king had to respect his position for life. Upon death, his successor had to confirm the magistrates in their offices. The principle of irremovability was reinforced by the system of venality and hereditary transmission.[23] These three notions lent a sense of complete security to the magistrates.

Consequently, judges had great independence as a counter to the king. During the eighteenth century, magistrates of the different parliaments, especially those belonging to the Parliament of Paris, took advantage of this situation and exceeded their traditional role of dispensing justice and regulating judicial matters. They misused their right of remonstrance to resist the king. Such defiance was possible, since the magistrates in the parliaments were called "counsellors of the king" and were an emanation of the ancient *Curia Regis*. As such, the judges believed in their right to advise the king on each royal ordinance, and they did so when an ordinance was presented to parliament for registration. If they disapproved of the text, they conveyed their objections *(remontrances)* to the king, who remained absolutely free either to heed or to ignore their challenges. A type of duel between the king and parliament would ensue when the monarch disregarded their advice and presented the identical ordinance to be registered a second time. Even though the king retained the final word, his authority was disputed and, consequently, diminished when he presided at parliament and ordered the registration. The magistrates of the parliaments used this practice to expand illegally the judicial power, by usurping the legislative power of the king. Thus, the judges developed a political opposition. The arrogance of these magistrates is explicable only through the principle of irremovability.

The king, of course, could exile the magistrates, but only temporarily. Otherwise, justice on appeal would have been suspended. In the second half of the eighteenth century, conflicts between the Crown and the parliaments were so frequent and so intense that Chancellor Maupeou, in collaboration with King Louis XV, concluded that radical reform was necessary. In 1771 he suppressed venality in the parliaments and repurchased the offices of the offending magistrates, to the amazement of the officeholders.[24] This permitted the parliaments to be reconstituted and staffed with magistrates devoted to the monarchy. Unfortunately when Louis XV died in 1774, his successor, Louis XVI, reintegrated the dismissed magistrates, who returned in triumph and continued until the Revolution to oppose all royal reform initiatives.

All new judges entered the profession knowing precisely the obligations and prerogatives that corresponded to the office they had purchased. In the *Ancien Régime*, becoming a royal judge was, in itself, a goal. In general, the person who bought an office was content to serve in that capacity until death, as there was no age limit.[25] A consequence, therefore, was that there was no notion of career in the system of venality. Nonetheless, for those who were ambitious, ascension to higher positions, either in the magistrature or in a more political field, was possible. The word career, from this perspective, should be used with caution.

Ambitious magistrates in a parliament could choose either to rise in the parliamentary world or to leave it. In the parliamentary arena a counsellor might aspire to become president of a division in his court of justice or even to become *président à mortier*. The sole requirement for such advancement was finding a vacant office. This was not always an easy task, and sometimes, if the counsellor had the opportunity, he might buy the office he was seeking in another parliament. The Prosecution Department was strictly hierarchical, and there, too, a promotion was realized through the purchase of a superior office. One could also shift from the bench to the Prosecution Department and *vice versa* to further career ambitions.

If a magistrate were to leave the parliament, generally his motivation was to buy the expensive office of *maître des requêtes* in the king's council. During the eighteenth century this class of office was regarded as a juncture; it still belonged to the judicial world, but it also opened doors to governmental responsibilities. One point is consistent in all of these examples: the judge managed his own career. Only two factors really affected his career decisions: his financial resources and the availability of a vacant office. He acted with total independence. Only if he wished to embark on a political career was the king's favor necessary.

A young *maître des requêtes* seeking a career in the political field would make every effort to be recognized by the king, for then he might be eligible for nomination to the office of *intendant*, the king's agent in a province. As such he would represent the king and assume responsibility for relations between the province and the sovereign. If he were to be successful, he might well end his career as a counsellor in the king's council. This was a prestigious position, although financially not particularly desirable. A successful *intendant* might also be chosen as secretary of state. However, this career path could be circumvented, as some magistrates left the parliament directly to become secretaries of state. Such promotions always raised the obvious questions of potential intrigues. From 1717 to 1789 thirty of the most notable political personalities came from the Parliament of Paris. Some were counsellors, and others were analogous to the secretaries of state to the financial, foreign affairs, marine, war, and interior departments.[26]

The system of venality practiced in the *Ancien Régime* tends to offend contemporary notions of ethics and propriety. Making the judiciary a private affair—whatever the reason—was not necessarily positive for the state, but was certainly viewed as advantageous for the judge. The system of venality fostered social mobility and, above all, assured total judicial independence.

Eighteenth-Century Assessments of the System of Venality

After 1750 France entered a particularly rich period, a dynamic era of fresh ideas and approaches. The philosophers of that time were critical of many institutions and proposed new standards for running the government. Their opinions of the system of venality are particularly interesting, but more important is the extent to which their writings had an impact on the public. Their influence can best be measured by examining the *cahiers de doléances* of 1789.

The philosophers of the eighteenth century were acutely conscious of various problems in the system for dispensation of justice. The necessity of reforming the criminal justice system was foremost in their minds. In addition, however, three essential aspects of the judicial system were considered to be of major consequence: the principle of venality, the role of the judge, and the qualifications for judges.

Montesquieu and Voltaire are representative of two distinct perspectives on the principle of venality. Montesquieu favored the system when he wrote *The Spirit of the Laws* (*L'Esprit des lois*)[27] but likewise acknowledged the reality, in the *Lettres persanes*,[28] that more than one judge had been forced to borrow the money to purchase the office and could even have faced financial ruin in the process. Montesquieu's position is understandable in that he had been a counsellor and, later, a *président à mortier* in the Parliament of Bordeaux. In 1726 he had abandoned the office,[29] but there was an almost reflex action to defend an institution to which he had once belonged and a system that he had accepted.

Montesquieu's writings, therefore, provided a simple avenue for Voltaire to attack. In *Commentaire sur quelques principales maximes de l'Esprit des lois*,[30] *Dictionnaire philosophique*,[31] and *Dialogues entre A, B, C*,[32] Voltaire expressed his amazement that Montesquieu would dishonor his own earlier career in his writings. Of course, Montesquieu had but inherited his uncle's office. Was this not reason for forgiveness? Leaving aside the personal attack, Voltaire was also critical of the system of venality in general, both in *Dictionnaire philosophique*[33] and in *Le Siècle de Louis XIV*.[34] He considered the practice of selling judges' offices to be an insult to the throne. He likened the practice to the prostitution of justice. He asserted that the system of venality had even raised the price of spices. For these reasons Voltaire applauded in *L'Equivoque* when Maupeou succeeded in reforming the parliament in 1771. His enemies claimed that his admiration was feigned solely to gain favor in court. Voltaire answered these accusations on April 20, 1772, in *Sur un écrit anonyme . . .* [35] and did not waver.[36]

When Montesquieu described his view of separation of powers in his chapter on the English constitution in *The Spirit of the Laws*,[37] he defined the judicial power and compared it to "*la bouche . . . de la loi, des êtres inanimés*," "the mouth of the law, dead beings." The general interpretation was that Montesquieu desired less powerful judges, judges who would behave like automatons, simply applying the law without liberty to interpret or initiate. Actually this interpretation of Montesquieu's intent would be inconsistent with his analysis of the French parliaments. In these sections of his writings Montesquieu appears to advocate emancipated judges, ones who could play an important role in questions of public law.[38] This latter understanding is more congruent with Montesquieu's position on the magistrates. He also insisted that, as a direct consequence of the separation of powers, the sovereign must not interfere directly with the magistrates in the exercise of their judicial authority.[39] Voltaire, on the other hand, in his *Fragments pour le prince royal de X*,[40] denounced the discretionary power granted to the judge. Rousseau, although not particularly interested in questions of judicial independence, suggested, in his theory of the supremacy of the law,[41] that judges should be in the service of the law and, therefore, should have a strictly limited field of action. In other words, neither Voltaire nor Rousseau would have endowed judicial officers with great independent judgment.

The role of judges is directly linked to the qualifications required of them. Voltaire had a keen interest in the criminal justice field and, in that context, contemplated the desirable qualities of a judge. His conclusions, which are found in the *Traité sur la tolérance à l'occasion de la mort de Jean Calas* and the *Commentaire sur le livre des délits et des peines par un avocat de province*, would apply equally to criminal or civil systems. Voltaire suggested that a judge should be a strong person capable of resisting all external influences; he should not be ambitious and, therefore, not unscrupulous; and he should be impartial and ready to recognize and correct his own errors. Judges of this caliber would honor the magistrature.[42] Rousseau, however, contended that common sense was the only criterion for one to be a good judge.[43]

Montesquieu, Voltaire, and Rousseau were read primarily by the cultivated members of the nobility and by the *bourgeoisie*. They were discussed in the *salons* and in the literary societies in the provinces. Was this sufficient exposure to have a real influence, a concrete impact, on the reforms that were requested at the end of the *Ancien Régime*? The answer lies in the *cahiers de doléances* of 1789.

The Cahiers De Doléances of 1789

The *cahiers de doléances* were not intended to cause a revolution, but rather were designed to reform the main institutions of the existing government, which were the objects of discontent. Among these was the judicial system. The notion of separation of powers was not, at this time, largely developed or accepted. Occasionally a *cahier* did, however, make reference to the principle.[44] Complaints largely rested on other grounds, and criticisms of the system of venality were very general but nevertheless adequate to make requests to end such a persistent system.[45] The authors of the *cahiers* envisioned a wholly new form of magistrature.[46] The primary difference between the positions of the *cahiers* and the philosophers was that the *cahiers* focused on concrete reforms in lieu of abstract concepts. The *cahiers* directly addressed the nature of systems that could replace the principle of venality,[47] the remuneration of the judges, and qualifications and functions (*statut*).

Two specific schemes were proposed from time to time for selecting the counsellors in the courts of parliament. One was a competitive examination, accessible only to judges and lawyers who had exercised their functions for a specified number of years. Promotion based on seniority was the second. Judges of the lower jurisdictions would be able to aspire to superior courts. Nevertheless the election of judges was the preferred system. Election was the solution praised by all who considered three independent powers in a state to be necessary and, consequently, a judicial power independent from the executive.[48]

On the general theme of election, at least for purposes of nomination, many variations were possible. The *cahiers* primarily advocated three potential methods that would apply equally to the judges of the lower jurisdictions and to those in the parliaments. A few supported direct election by the voters. More often, though, they proposed a system based on designation through the established assemblies, such as the provincial assemblies.[49] The last proposal was that the jurisdictions in general or any assembly composed of their members could present, or even appoint, the judges. This would amount to co-optation. None of the proposed systems totally excluded the king's participation. Several candidates would always be presented to the king for him to name one. Moreover, he would appoint directly the members of the Prosecution Department and the presidents—at least the first president—in each parliament.

The qualifications requested were designed to ensure competent jurists, without reference to social barriers. Judges belonging to the lower jurisdictions would be evaluated only on knowledge and merit, regardless of their social origins. The lawyers corresponded with this conception. For this reason the *cahiers* concluded that the judges of the lower jurisdictions would be chosen from among them. This was an obvious reaction against the practices of the *Ancien Régime* and the resulting judicial dynasties. In the parliaments another criterion was added, that of respectability. Here the candidates could be recruited from either lawyers or judges. The *cahiers* further proposed that the counsellors should not be too young (thirty was regarded as the minimum age to be a counsellor), which was another reaction against earlier practices. A more popular point of view was that members of the *Tiers Etat* (Third Estate, or common people) should be admitted as judges in the lower jurisdictions and in the parliaments. There was also some sentiment expressed that recruitment of jurists should be at the provincial rather than the national level.

Attracting desirable candidates for the office would be necessary under any of the proposed systems. One means of accomplishing this was to make the position financially secure. Three institutions of the *Ancien Régime* were reviewed to determine the remuneration of judges[50]—the spices, wages, and retirement pensions. Some *cahiers* accepted that the spices should be maintained if their amount were reduced and regulated, but most demanded their elimination. The principle of the gratuity of justice was requested. The spice system was viewed further as humiliating for the judges and incompatible with their dignity.

Judges, therefore, would have to be paid a reasonable living wage. Some *cahiers* suggested that wages should be in proportion to the work accomplished and that assisting at a trial could serve as the basis. The primary question debated was who would pay the wages. The obligation could be that of the provinces—which would correspond with the concept of a provincial magistrature—or it might be an obligation of the central government.

The system of elections did not, in practice, deter people from seeking the office of judge for years. A decent salary should have been a sufficient inducement to attract candidates. Some *cahiers* thought this was not enough and adopted quite a modern concept by proposing that an "honest pension" be paid when the judge retired—50 percent of his wages after twenty-five years of service. The idea of paying a pension was not revolutionary in itself. What was novel was that pensions would be an obligation for the state, whereas before, pensions had depended on the king's favor.

Money was not the only inducement to attract people to a judicial vocation. The assurance of a firm definition of the office and its tenure was equally important.[51] The authors of the *cahiers* regarded the principle of irremovability of a judge to be essential. They managed to reconcile this proposition with the system of elections by providing that once elected, a judge was irremovable during his term of office. Thus the will of the majority would constitute the judicial power, totally independent from the executive.

Furthermore, authors of the *cahiers* felt that offering an honorific position would attract able candidates. They proposed granting personal nobility to judges, by addressing letters conferring the quality of veteran and an honorary title at the end of a long tenure. In short, the *cahiers de doléances* were, in many respects, reactions against the practices of the *Ancien Régime*. The proposals proffered seemed concrete and reasonable, as their intent was to create a magistrature where only "merits, talents, virtue"[52] would have a place.

THE FRENCH REVOLUTION

The *Etats Généraux* (States-General) gathered solemnly in Versailles on May 5, 1789 (see Table 3.1). The body was composed of 1,155 deputies, of whom almost 50 percent were members of the legal profession (magistrates, lawyers, public notaries, or solicitors). They were fully conscious of the irreversible consequences of all their decisions, as they were well versed in the law. On June 17, 1789, they declared themselves the National Assembly *Constituante*, or an assembly convened to write a constitution.[53] They were interested not only in changing the political institutions of government, but also in restructuring the judicial organization. In this particular field the deputies wavered for months between a reformist and a revolutionary attitude. During the famous night session of August 4, 1789, the assembly voted abolition of the venality system and the principle of reimbursement of the offices. That night they also voted to suppress the use of spices and proclaimed the gratuity of justice.[54] These two decisions were quite significant, as they both were indictments of the established system. Nonetheless the judges of the *Ancien Régime* were to be retained, at least until new judges were designated. The exception was the parliaments, which were considered to be politically too dangerous to continue. Therefore, the parliaments were ordered to cease their functions during the autumn of 1790. Several deputies noted that the French national treasury was in no condition to reimburse these offices. That consideration was set aside,[55] and on March 24, 1790, the deputies of the *Constituante* voted for a complete reorganization of the judicial system. It was a total break with the system of the *Ancien Régime*.[56] In this context, the concept of the role and function of a judge was bound to change.

The deputies of the *Constituante* were influenced by the ideas of Montesquieu, Voltaire, and Rousseau, as well as by the proposals in the *cahiers de doléances*. As the Revolution advanced and war was declared, the assembly feared the betrayal of the king and a reaction by the aristocrats. And economic conditions worsened. When the third national assembly—the Convention—was elected, the deputies had a totally different view of the judicial organization. They regarded the role of judges from a political perspective. The government of the *Directoire* had the same attitude.

Table 3.1
The End of the Monarchy and the French Revolution (1789–1799)

REGIME	ASSEMBLY	DATES	CONSTITUTION
Monarchy King Louis XVI	Reunion of Etats Généraux transformed into	May 1789	
	National Assembly Constituante	June, 1789 to September 30, 1791	Constitution of September 3, 1791
suspended on August 10, 1792	Législative	October 1, 1791 to September 20, 1792	
First Republic	Convention	September 21, 1792 to October 26, 1795	Constitution of June 24, 1793 (never applied)
	Directoire	August, 1795 to November, 1799	Constitution of fructidor 5, Third year of the Republic (August 22, 1795)

Judges in a Legal Utopia

Those in the legal profession desired ideal judges and a type of legal utopia. The deputies debated the principle theories advanced before the Revolution concerning the judicial organization. These discussions led them inevitably to envision a new type of judge, with a very different profile. The debates were numerous but centered on two basic themes inspired, more or less, by Rousseau and Montesquieu. On one hand, Rousseau had contended that every man had the capacity to administer justice. Montesquieu, on the other hand, had raised the issue of whether there was simply a judicial function as opposed to an inherent judicial power.

The first issue, that of every man's ability to administer justice, was based on the belief that justice should be a question of common sense and should not be reserved to few persons of legal professions. In the basic decree of August 16-24, 1790, the *Constituante* defined three classifications of judges serving in civil courts: arbitrators, justices of the peace, and district judges. The same judges also served for the criminal courts. The decree of April 30, 1790, did, however, introduce juries into criminal courts in France. The question of placing a jurisdiction at the pinnacle of the judicial organization was vigorously discussed. Some deputies feared an institution of influence like the ancient parliaments. They also considered such an institution to be useless, since judges could only apply the law, without interpretation. In case of difficulty judges were to refer the issue to the legislator. Others thought a superior tribunal to be necessary to control the decisions *a posteriori*. The conclusion of these deliberations was the decree of November 27—December 1, 1790, which created the *tribunal de cassation*.

Not all of the newly created judgeships were to be selected in the same fashion; some were elected but not others. The elected judges were the justices of the peace, the district judges, and the judges *en cassation*.[57] The system of election corresponded to the revolutionary ideology proclaimed in the Declaration of the Rights of Man and Citizen of 1789. All power emanated from the nation; election of public officials was the only way for the citizens to confer power. In this general context the principle of electing judges was passed unanimously on May 5, 1790. The question of the length of tenure for jurists divided the Assembly, as this issue was linked to the principle of irremovability. Election for life was consistent with the principle of irremovability, but such a solution was not without risk. Such a proposal was reminiscent of the *Ancien Régime*. The judge would assume his position, appear as a professional, and slip into a routine, whereby he would lose interest in remaining current on the law and be tempted to create instead a personal jurisprudence. The magistrates of the *Ancien Régime*, sitting in the National Assembly as deputies, were formally opposed to such a situation, and as a consequence, the discussion tended to favor limited tenure. The lawyers sitting as deputies spoke in favor of a relatively long term—three, four, six, eight, or even ten years—in order to give the judge a certain stability and enable him to acquire experience. Finally, the *Assemblée Constituante* voted for terms of two years for the justices of the peace, four years for the judges *en cassation*, and six years for the district judges. It was also decided that at the end of each term, the judges could be reelected immediately, since few citizens were qualified to be judges and since decisions could not be made by a single judge.[58] To provide a guarantee for the judges, the principle of irremovability was acknowledged during one's term of office, although the concept remained controversial because of potential prerogatives.

The nature of the elections for judges requires explanation, as it was not a straightforward process. First, not all citizens were permitted to vote, as the law distinguished between active and passive citizens. Each Frenchman of twenty-five years of age, domiciled one year in a canton (the smallest administrative unit), and paying a special tax (equivalent to three days' pay) was an active citizen, so long as he was not a servant, bankrupt, or insolvent. The active citizens in each canton composed the primary assembly designed to elect directly the justices of the peace and the citizens constituting the electoral assembly of the district (the second administrative unit). The citizens composing the district assembly were in proportion of one second-degree elector for every 100 active citizens. To be a second-degree elector, one was required to pay a special tax equivalent to ten days' pay. The electoral assembly of the district elected the district judges. The second-degree electors of the entire department (the third administrative unit) elected the judges *en cassation*. In essence, therefore, judges were indirectly elected and only by citizens having a certain wealth or income.

The prerequisites to stand as a candidate for a judgeship were also changed. Religion was no longer of consequence, as Protestants and Jews, as well as Catholics, were permitted to seek the office. To become a justice of the peace, a district judge, or a judge *en cassation*, a candidate was required to be at least thirty years old and to pay a special tax equal to ten days' pay. The difference among the three types of judgeships rested on the prior training required. For example, the justice of the peace was inspired by similar Dutch and English institutions that had been praised by Voltaire. The objective of this judge was to reconcile the litigants in specific categories of cases, thus avoiding lawsuits.[59] A sense of equity was far more important than legal knowledge, which was not required. In contrast, district judges and judges *en cassation* had to know the law. A diploma was not required, as the level of studies in the law faculties was very limited at that time. Nevertheless there were requirements of experience in the practice of law—five years for a district judge and ten years for a judge *en cassation*. This experience could be as a judge, as a member of the Prosecution Department, as a professor in a law faculty, or as a lawyer. The sole restriction was that members of the clergy were barred from the judiciary.

The deputies were perhaps surprised by their own audacity in deciding to have all judges elected. The contrast with their treatment of selecting members to the Prosecution Department can be seen as a clear example of the deputies' uncertainty. Initially, on May 8, 1790, the deputies decided that the king would name members of the Prosecution Department, who would have life tenure. Distrust of the king, however, prompted the deputies to moderate this position by dividing the functions of the Prosecution Department. The *commissaire du Roi* was created as the office responsible for sanctions. He would be named by the king. The *accusateur public*, on the other hand, would be responsible for presenting to the jury of judgment the charges admitted by the jury of accusation. He would, like judges, be elected for renewable six-year terms. This was passed on August 4, 1790, and undoubtedly resulted in a weakening of the Prosecution Department.

The other officials charged with dispensing justice were to be named variously. For example, the arbitrators[60] were considered to be judges. Any person having his own free will and legal capacity could be chosen by the litigants as an arbitrator. The issue was one of confidence. This procedure was a perfect expression of Rousseau's concept that anyone was capable of finding an equitable solution, even if the solution lay on the margin of the legal system. The decision made by the arbitrator was taken in the first instance. An arbitrator could be requested in civil affairs but was obligatory in family matters or cases in which the parties were close members of a family.

The other revolutionary innovation, borrowed from the British, was the institution of juries.[61] Some deputies, among them Duport and Robespierre, proposed establishment of juries in both civil and criminal cases. This proposal met with violent opposition, primarily from law practitioners. Objections were based on issues of the rules of evidence. In England the system was possible because testimonial proof was allowed; in France it was not, as proof was mainly written. In the end the jury was accepted only in criminal cases. Members of the jury were to be ordinary people, drawn from a list of thirty persons compiled for each department by an agent of the government. To be registered on this list, an individual had to be owner or life tenant of real estate, assessed on the tax roles for a sum equivalent to 200 days' pay for residents of cities with more than 6,000 population and 150 days' pay for residents of smaller cities. Jurors were to be chosen from this list by lots. Again, wealth was the obvious basis of the system. Juries played a far more important role during the revolution than now. The jury of accusation was akin to the English grand jury, was composed of eight citizens, and decided whether to prosecute or not. The jury of judgment (the English *petit* jury) had twelve citizens and decided guilt or innocence.

All the above elements provide a reasonable description of the judge in the largest sense of the word, but the information would be incomplete if the *Constituante's* position on the role of the judiciary was not considered. Debates on the question of the role of the judiciary appeared in more than one way as the key element in the development of a new regime. The meaning of each theory[62] and the practical consequence for the judges are logical questions.

Montesquieu's theory of separation of powers must be accepted as the starting point. As discussed earlier, in 1789 some accepted the concept of three powers in government, whereas others envisioned only two. If the judiciary were to be a power in government, then it would have equal standing with the executive and the legislative power and, as such, have its roots in national sovereignty. Curiously, many deputies using the expression "separation of powers" did not fully comprehend the implications and rather designed various means of limiting judicial power. Attitudes of the deputies essentially marked rejection of the judicial organization of the past, in particular the strong power exerted by the parliaments. Other deputies supportive of the monarchy, like Cazalès, preferred a judicial function integrated with the executive power, and thereby in a position of dependency. These deputies persisted in asserting that the king was the supreme judge in the nation. These two positions were fundamental because each was the basis of a different answer to the question of whether or not elected judges would be appointed by the king, as was the rule before the Revolution. Those who believed that the judiciary was a function dependent on the executive power reaffirmed that the function must be administered in the king's name. They fully trusted the king and demanded that the appointment of the judges—even though elected—be recognized as a royal prerogative. They attempted to persuade the Assembly that adopting any other position would be conspiring against the monarchy. Many deputies, nevertheless, argued against this position. The deputies in opposition no longer wanted an absolute monarchy (Barnave), for if the king could refuse a judge, he would hold in his hands the judicial power (Lameth). They mistrusted less the king than his advisors, and they feared that the political practices of the *Ancien Régime* would flourish again. But some, such as Roederer, did not want their attitude to be interpreted as disloyalty to the monarchy. La Révellière de Lépeaux suggested that recognition of a national right to designate judges without the power to appoint them was illogical. That the nation was the source of all power and had an uncontested right to appoint was argued by Mougins de Roquefort. The debates did not turn in favor of the king. In a desperate attempt to maintain a shade of royal authority, Cazalès proposed that three candidates be presented to the king from whom he would choose one. On May 7, 1790, the *Constituante* voted that the king could not refuse to appoint the judge presented to him and that only one name would be submitted. In making this decision the Assembly said, in essence, that the judge was effectively an emanation of the people and that the judiciary was a power in itself, albeit a limited power.

Every possible measure was taken to avoid a strong judicial power.[63] The preliminary question thereafter seems to have been whether the judges should be itinerant (in imitation of English institutions) or stationary. If the judges were not settled, they had less authority but seemed to be at the total disposal of the population. Having judges who moved from place to place was viewed as a guarantee of impartiality and incorruptibility. Duport even considered that there should be simply judges without jurisdictions. Such an "advantageous" arrangement might prove, however, to be more illusion than reality. Itinerant judges would have constant opportunities for entertaining themselves in a manner not compatible with their function. On May 1, 1790, the *Constituante* voted for the general principle of stationary judges, and on August 13, the Assembly applied the same rule to the *tribunal de cassation*. Despite the wisdom of this decision there was concern that it not result in re-emergence of the great parliaments of the *Ancien Régime*. Perhaps that explains why the deputies were attentive to limiting the number of judges. They also abolished all hierarchy, by providing that the district judges would be judges of appeal for neighboring jurisdictions. They further limited the judges' role to a strictly jurisprudential field by forbidding any interpretation or completion of the law. Participation by judges in political issues was firmly denied. The result was a real diminution of the judicial power in comparison with what it had been before the Revolution.

With these restrictions in mind, there remained concern about the type of person who would seek a judgeship. The electoral proceedings began in mid-October 1790 and lasted for several months, since they occurred on two levels. The new judges assumed their positions on January 25, 1791. Studies have not been made on the justices of the peace and arbitrators elected, so we know little about their characteristics. The first elections to take place concerned the district judges.[64] In Paris the men elected were very competent. Most of them had exercised judicial functions before the Revolution, as magistrates in Parliament, in lower royal jurisdictions, or as lawyers. Some of these veterans were actually deputies in the National Assembly and had demonstrated their abilities during debates on the reorganization of the judicial system. They were regarded as the best to try the new system. In the provinces the results were not equally positive, perhaps because capable persons were not as easy to find as they were in the capital. In some towns, like Agen in the Southwest and Lille and Arras in the North, the choice was in favor of people who had been judges in the *Ancien Régime*. In Brittany primarily lawyers were elected. In some towns, like Versailles, new men emerged, ones with political ambitions, like Robespierre. Incidentally, because of his political ambitions, he quickly resigned and never served as a judge. The election of the judges of the *tribunal de cassation* in March 1791 resulted in a similar tendency.[65] The choices were competent people, including several deputies of the *Constituante* (sixteen out of the forty-two elected).

The dangers of politization that might have been a consequence of the electoral system were apparently non-existent. On the whole the electors, as well as the candidates, acted rationally and named good jurists. The politicians had two main interests in the results of the elections. They were anxious to know if the system they had created was likely to endure and if the judges selected under the system would take their assignments seriously.

Assessments of the system itself were varied.[66] The former deputy Thouret, in his position as an active participant in the elaboration of the new system and as a newly selected district judge, expressed his satisfaction to the Assembly on May 10, 1792. He explained that the new organization functioned without serious difficulty. Some judges had exceeded their powers and taken regulations; but, after all, past habits were difficult to break. Nonetheless he was optimistic and asserted that such mistakes would not be repeated. Chasset, judge of the *tribunal de cassation* and deputy at the Convention, was not as enthusiastic when he addressed the Third National Assembly on September 22, 1792. He related that every day the *tribunal de cassation* received judgments that lacked common sense. This, he contended, was because the judges were scattered all over the territory, and in small localities capable men were rare.

Two ministers of justice, at one-month intervals, formulated their assessments of the judges.[67] Joly proclaimed his indignation to the Legislative Assembly on July 9, 1792. The justices of the peace, especially those in the country, he explained, lacked punctuality and rigor. They had obviously accepted the positions without any interest in the institution's benefiting the population. The assistant judges did not come when they were needed. These criticisms were of the judges' non-professional attitudes, not of the system itself. Danton then wrote on August 19, 1792, that the judges who had been elected were men of the past, who had adapted to the new system but who had no sincere attachment to the Revolution. He concluded his comments on the renewal of the judges. The political turning point was reached.

The judges elected in 1790 were legally in office until expiration of their prescribed terms: 1792 for the justices of the peace; 1794 for the judges *en cassation*; 1796 for the district judges. But the suspension of King Louis XVI after the revolutionary tumult of August 10, 1792, the establishment of a temporary Executive Committee, and the ascension to power of men like Danton altered all events and expectations. The judicial organization so recently established was already in question, and the politicians had their own agenda.

Judges in the Politicians' View

Some politicians proposed suppression of the new organization. The majority of deputies intended to maintain the system but change the judges. Among the latter group was Danton, who wanted judges to be men of common sense. Actually, as a former lawyer at the king's counsel, he was well aware that such a qualification was not sufficient to handle properly delicate legal issues, but as a shrewd politician he recognized the necessity of placing men favorable to the Revolution everywhere possible. Such an aim was not easily accomplished.

Two approaches were possible to the policy of recruiting judges. Voting laws facilitating entrance into the magistrature was one that was to be practiced essentially by the Convention. Nominating the judges by the executive power was the other, which was mostly used under the *Directoire*.

On August 12, 1792, the *Législative* agreed to its' own dissolution. A new assembly, the Convention,[68] would be elected on a more equal basis.[69] The distinction between active and passive citizens would be abolished, and universal suffrage established. All

Frenchmen of twenty-one years of age, domiciled one year, living from their own revenues or salaries (as long as they were not servants) had the right to vote and to constitute the primary assemblies. Citizens aged twenty-five and over were eligible to serve in the electoral assemblies. These requirements were applicable to both political and judicial elections.

The Convention decided on September 22, 1792, that judges could be chosen from among the citizens that were age twenty-five, without any requirement of legal knowledge. Attainment of the age of twenty-five was also the only requirement for jurors, according to the decrees of August 16, 1793, and *nivôse* 5, second year of the Republic[70] (December 25, 1793). All these decisions opened a wide access to the magistrature.[71]

The constitution of the *Directoire* of *fructidor* 5, third year of the Republic (August 22, 1795), was not as absolute. It appeared in more than one way to be a constitution of transition by degrees.[72] The constitution simplified the judicial organization by providing that in the main town of each department, there would be only one jurisdiction staffed by at least twenty judges and five assistant judges. The arbitrator in family matters was eliminated. The constitution addressed the requirements for a judge and settled on a synthesis of the systems of 1790 and 1792. As in 1790, the judges would be elected, but for five-year instead of six-year renewable terms. The distinction between active and passive citizens was reintroduced. In other words, all Frenchmen, as long as they paid a "contribution," whatever the amount, were first-degree electors and composed the primary assemblies. Second-degree electors were those who had an income of 150 or 200 days' pay. The proportion was one second-degree elector for every 200 active citizens. The initial condition, so seemingly reasonable in itself, biased the final result. The system was far more severe than the one created in 1790, and the electors were half as numerous. But on the other hand, as in 1792, there was no condition of legal knowledge for judicial candidates. The regime had confidence in a wealthy judge, regardless of his education. The Prosecution Department was represented by one *commissaire* and one substitute, both appointed and removable by the executive power. Even when the conditions to be elected and the logical consequences thereof had been considered, the elections always brought surprises, which failed to correspond with the government's wish. Appointment by the executive power appeared, then, as a more effective control of judicial personnel.

The political events of the spring of 1793 aroused a climate of fear and suspicion. The deputies declared *la Patrie en danger* (a national emergency) and instituted severe controls on all citizens. In this general context the judges had to respond to the political exigency of the Convention, even more during the *Directoire*. The executive power was seen as the necessary means to accomplish desired aims. Thus began the erosion of the electoral system in favor of executive appointment.

On March 10, 1793, the Convention created the Revolutionary Tribunal sitting in Paris to judge all anti-revolutionary enterprises and conspiracies against the state.[73] The tribunal was composed of five judges, twelve jurors, one public prosecutor, and two substitutes, all of whom were nominated by the Convention on the proposal of the *Comité de Sûreté Générale* and the *Comité de Salut Public.*[74] When the decree was discussed in the assembly, Cambon criticized the principle of appointment and explained the potential dangers. Cambon feared that the government would make mistakes and grant power to unscrupulous and ambitious men who would sell their integrity, and thus would not serve the revolutionary cause. His pleas were not heeded then or later. Rather, the Assembly passed the decrees of October 7, 1793, February 19, 1794, and March 13, 1794, enabling appointment for all judicial vacancies without elections.[75] The *tribunal de cassation*, although it was considered separately, suffered the same fate with the decree of September 29, 1793. The judges who were replaced had generally been tried before the Revolutionary Tribunal.

Motivations were different under the *Directoire*, but the policy was the same, a policy that was continued even more intensively.[76] The law of *frimaire* 22, fourth year of the Republic (December 13, 1795), authorized the executive to name judges to fill vacancies until the next scheduled elections. These vacancies were created in different ways. Elections had just taken place, and some new judges were declared ineligible because they had emigrated, were members of the family of an emigrant, or were ex-nobles. In some departments the electoral procedure was avoided, so that no judges had been elected. In other cases the judges resigned because their salaries were not paid regularly. The *Directoire* wanted reliable men. Therefore, it required that new judges be chosen from among citizens having already held public offices. That law was abrogated by the law of *germinal* 30, fifth year of the Republic (April 19, 1797), which provided that the jurisdictions could fill vacancies on the courts themselves. After the general elections of April 1797, several results were annulled for political reasons, and the law of *fructidor* 19, fifth year of the Republic (September 5, 1797), returned to the executive the right to appoint judges unrestricted by any requirements.

All of these various schemes were created to reflect the political goals of the assemblies. There is the question of how satisfactory the results were. One month after passing the electoral reform the Convention decided to renew all judicial personnel, with the exception of the members of the *tribunal de cassation.*[77] The decree of October 19-20, 1792, related to the justices of the peace, the judges in the civil, criminal, and commercial jurisdictions, and the public prosecutors. The elections took place at the beginning of 1793. The results are surprising today but corresponded precisely to the Assembly's will of having ordinary men of common sense on the bench. The tribunals in the department of the Seine are a good example. These tribunals had few judges who had practiced law; the others had followed quite distinct professions. For instance, there was a painter, a carver, a gardener, an engraver, and a lapidary. There were even fewer who had been trained in law among the assistant judges. These included a wood merchant, a doctor, a hairdresser, and a carpenter. In all, of the fifty-one judges and assistant judges, only twenty-six had received legal training. Such results were appalling, but few people dared to express their opinions. Then, with the Reign of Terror at its height, additional judicial seats became vacant, especially in the *tribunal de cassation.* Applying the decrees of October 7, 1793, February 19, 1794, and March 13, 1794, the Convention appointed replacements directly. The choice was eclectic, with nominees ranging from an ex-president of the *Législative* assembly to a poet.

The reorganization of the judiciary by the Constitution of the *Directoire* necessitated new elections, which took place in the fourth year of the Republic (1796). The results expressed two opinions of the electors. The first was political—it was a reaction against the

Revolution, as many opponents, both moderate and royalist, were elected. The second element was a decided preference for judges having already practiced law. But as the *Directoire* was a period of repeated *coups d'état*, the judges never served the duration of their mandate and elections occurred every year. In the fifth year of the Republic (April 1797) the royalists obtained even greater electoral support. This success worried the *Directoire* and probably explains the subsequent law of *fructidor* 19, fifth year of the Republic, and the appointment of men only of the government's political persuasion. In the elections of the sixth (April 1798) and seventh (April 1799) years of the Republic 50 percent of the judges selected were republicans. Again, as before, the others were replaced by left-wing personalities. The obvious conclusion was that the *Directoire* was interested primarily in political considerations and not concerned with the aptitude of judges. Perhaps even more symptomatic of this trend was the decision, after the first victories of the revolutionary armies and the conquests in the North in the fourth year of the Republic, that foreigners could enter the ranks of the French magistrature without being naturalized. Such was the case with Busschop, a native of Bruzes, who became a judge in the tribunal of the department of the Lys on *frimaire* 7, fourth year of the Republic (November 28, 1795). Generally, some of the judges were effective technicians, but not all, which led to complaints, especially in the provinces.[78]

Undoubtedly the Revolution changed the face of the judiciary. The only point in common between judges of the Revolution and those of earlier eras was the oath at the beginning of the mandate.[79] Otherwise, the entire concept of who or what was a judge was different. The judges were not professionals, and if jurists were elected in the early years of the Revolution, the situation changed dramatically as the Convention introduced politics as a primary criterion. Envisioning the situation of a judge with a view toward a career is almost impossible. Notions of a career were hampered by the electoral system; political interferences; the absence of a hierarchy, which eludes all prospect of advancement; and low and irregularly paid salaries.[80] The position of judge seemed to be destined only for people devoted to the public cause. The decree of June 26, 1793,[81] obliged judges to give their opinions aloud in the courtroom, and more than one, motivated by fear, was inclined to satisfy the auditors and not to decide in conformity with his conscience. Such behavior would hardly be consistent with devotion to public service.

The experiences of the French Revolution did not correspond precisely to the hopes of 1789. The judges who were elected deserve some tribute. Happily they were mainly moderates who worked in good accord with those judges named by the executive.[82] Progressively political considerations pushed aside the electoral system in favor of a system of appointment. The *Directoire* is regarded as having accustomed the population to a new system, that of appointment, which would later be established by the *Consulat*.

NOTES

1. The expression *lettre de cachet*, or sealed letter, is the opposite of another type of letter written by the king, the *lettres patentes*, which were never closed. The *lettres de cachet* were countersigned by a secretary of state and had different uses, in particular personal and administrative correspondence and orders to arrest someone.

2. There are two exceptions to this general rule. In the parliaments (royal jurisdictions that correspond to current courts of appeal), the functions of the first president and the head of the Prosecution Department could only be conferred by the king. In the consular jurisdictions (royal jurisdictions created to judge commercial affairs) all judges were elected by merchants.

3. Roland Mousnier, *Les Institutions de la France sous la monarchie absolue* (Paris: P.U.F., 1980), vol. I, pp. 38-60.

4. Marcel Rousselet, *Histoire de la magistrature française des origines à nos jours* (Paris: Plon, 1957), vol. I, pp. 97 ff.

5. Pierre Villard, *Les Justices seigneuriales dans la Marche* (Paris: L.G.D.J., 1969), p. 140.

6. The price is mentioned in the receipt of liquidation of March 21, 1791, when the owner, Dionis du Séjour, was reimbursed by the State. *Minutier Central, XLIX*, 888.

7. Villard, p. 139.

8. Raoul Aubin, *L'Organisation judiciaire d'après les Cahiers de 1789* (Paris: Jouve, 1928), pp. 113-15.

9. On grave occasions the king could call his *Etats Généraux*, the political assembly representing the entire nation. He then ordered the *baillis* (royal judges) to begin the procedure. Each *bailli* summoned in his town

the electoral assembly of each one of the three Orders—Clergy, Nobility and *Tiers Etat*. Each assembly elected its deputy and wrote a *cahier de doléances* containing the complaint addressed to the king and the remedies suggested. The calling of the *Etats Généraux* was an exceptional event. Near the end of the *Ancien Régime* there was one in 1614 and only one other, in 1789. François Oliver-Martin, *Histoire du Droit Français des origines à la Révolution* (Paris: Domat-Montchrestien, 1948), pp. 370-71, 375-76, 674-75.

10. Jean-Pierre Royer, *La Société judiciaire depuis le XVIIIe siècle* (Paris: P.U.F., 1979), pp. 44-47, 66-67.

11. Ibid., p. 65.

12. Rousselet, vol. I, p. 219.

13. The "nobility by the robe" is an expression designating those persons who acquired nobility by buying specific and expensive judicial offices. This system enabled them to pass from the *bourgeoisie* to the nobility. This nobility appeared during the seventeenth century and was very recent compared with the "nobility by the sword," which represented those who had acquired the nobility while fighting. These rather simple distinctions do not reflect all of the true complexities of the definitions. François Bluche, *Les Magistrats du Parlement de Paris au XVIIIe siècle (1715-1776)* (Paris: Les Belles Lettres, 1960), pp. 303-25.

14. Royer, pp. 36-37, 51; Rousselet, vol. I, p. 235.

15. Royer, p. 50.

16. Ibid., p. 41.

17. Ibid., p. 50.

18. Bluche, p. 171.

19. Aubin, p. 155; Rousselet, vol. II, p. 229; Royer, pp. 60-61.

20. Aubin, p. 155; Rousselet, vol. II, pp. 230-34; Royer, pp. 62-63.

21. Royer, p. 63.

22. Bluche, pp. 143-239.

23. Rousselet, vol. II, pp. 155-62.

24. Robert Villers, *L'organisation du Parlement de Paris et des conseils supérieurs d'après la réforme de Maupeou, 1771-1774* (Paris: Jouve, 1937).

25. The king tried at least to persuade infirm judges to abandon their positions, but as they had no retirement pension, they clung to their wages and spices. Rousselet, vol. II, pp. 205-8.

26. Royer, pp. 86-89.

27. *L'Esprit des lois*, Book V, Chapter 19 (1748).

28. Letter LXVI (1721).

29. Rousselet, vol. I, p. 113; Jean Dalat, *Montesquieu, magistrat*, in *Archives des lettres modernes*, ed. Lettres modernes (1971), p. 8.

30. Vol. 28, p. 399 (1777).

31. V° *Esprit des lois*, t. 41, p. 83.

32. *Premier entretien* (1768).

33. V° *Education*, t. 39, p. 1; V° *Gouvernement*, section 3, t. 40, p. 94; V° *Parlement de Paris*, section *Remontrances des Parlements*, t. 41, p. 346.

34. Chapter 25, t. 20, p. 121.

35. *Correspondance générale*, t. 47, p. 368.

36. Pierre Mille, *Voltaire et les institutions* (Reims, 1979), pp. 325-36.

37. Book XI, pp. 6, 49.

38. Karel Menzo Schönfeld, *Montesquieu: "en la bouche . . . de la loi"* (Leiden: New Rhine Publishers, 1979), pp. 75-76.

39. Rousselet, vol. I, pp. 37-38.

40. Jean Michel Barrué, *Voltaire et le droit pénal* (Paris, 1966), p. 354.

41. Hilla Limann, *Le Contrat social de Jean-Jacques Rousseau et son influence sur les constitutions de 1791 et 1793* (Paris, 1965), p. 76.

42. Barrué, pp. 356-57, 363.

43. Gérard Sautel, *Histoire des Institutions Publiques depuis la Révolution Française* (Paris: Dalloz, 1974), p. 148.

44. Aubin, pp. 14-15.

45. Ibid., pp. 27, 116.

46. Another proposal, as part of the restructuring of the judiciary, was the use of jurors in criminal trials. Jacques Godechot, *Les Institutions de la France sous la Révolution et l'Empire* (Paris: P.U.F., 1985), p. 142.

47. Aubin, pp. 120-47.

48. The smaller number defending the theory of two powers only—the legislative and the executive—declared that the judges should be named by the executive. Ibid., pp. 27-29.

49. At the end of the *Ancien Régime* all of the provinces of France did not benefit from the privilege of having assemblies called *états provinciaux*. They did not sit year round, but rather were summoned by the king for each meeting. The deputies that were elected represented the three orders (Clergy, Nobility, and *Tiers Etat*), on the model of the *Etats Généraux*.

50. Aubin, pp. 155-62.

51. Ibid., pp. 162-64.

52. Ibid., p. 165.

53. Godechot, p. 41.

54. Rousselet, vol. I, p. 116.

55. Indeed, the *Constituante* essentially (but also the succeeding revolutionary assemblies) passed a detailed legislation concerning reimbursement for judicial offices. This legislation stipulated the basis for evaluation of the offices, the procedure that had to be observed, and the creation of an entire administration in charge of this specific activity. The offices were

effectively reimbursed mainly in *assignates*. Jacqueline Lucienne Lafon, *Recherches sur la fin des juridictions d'Ancien Régime pendant la Révolution: Le Châtelet et le Parlement de Paris* (Paris, 1972).

56. Royer, pp. 175-76.

57. Rousselet, vol. I, pp. 124-29, 134-37, 140-41, and vol. II, p. 163; Royer, pp. 209-13, 215, 217-23; Sautel, pp. 155-56, 162-64.

58. The justice of the peace was assisted by two assessors. There were three district judges who decided cases in the first instance and four when acting as a court of last resort. The *tribunal de cassation* was composed of forty-one or forty-two judges, alternatively, because there was one judge for every two departments, and there were eighty-three departments in France since February 15, 1790.

59. The justice of the peace had no competence to decide cases involving real property. He could only hear personal actions contesting up to 50 pounds without appeal and 100 pounds in first instance.

60. Royer, pp. 180, 211-12; Sautel, pp. 154-55.

61. Rousselet, vol. I, pp. 117-19, 132-33; Royer, pp. 210-11.

62. Rousselet, vol. I, p. 123; Royer, pp. 176-80, 183-88.

63. Rousselet, vol. I, pp. 117-20, 139-40; vol. II, p. 365; Royer, pp. 179-81, 214.

64. Rousselet, vol. I, pp. 129-32; Royer, pp. 224-28.

65. Rousselet, vol. I, p. 141.

66. Ibid., vol. I, p. 144.

67. Royer, pp. 237-38.

68. "Convention" was the term used in imitation of the American Constitutional Convention.

69. Rousselet, vol. I, p. 146; Godechot, pp. 273-74.

70. The Convention gathered for the first time on September 21, 1792, and abolished the monarchy. On the next day the assembly decided that the first year of the Republic would begin on September 21, 1792. The political rupture with the past was officially proclaimed. Soon the deputies went even further and rejected the Gregorian calendar, which was, they thought, a symbol of Christianity. A revolutionary calendar was adopted by the decrees of October 5, 1793, and *frimaire* 4, second year of the Republic (November 24, 1793). It remained in force until *nivôse* 10, fourteenth year of the Republic (December 31, 1805). Godechot, pp. 275, 423-26, 764.

71. Rousselet, vol. I, pp. 145, 148.

72. Ibid., vol. I, p. 154; Royer, p. 241; Sautel, pp. 226, 310.

73. Godechot, pp. 376-88; Rousselet, vol. I, pp. 148-52; Royer, pp. 240-41; Sautel, pp. 170-71.

74. In September 1793 the *Tribunal Révolutionnaire* was so active that

it required more personnel. There were sixteen judges, sixty members of the jury, and five substitutes. After the overthrow of Robespierre (*thermidor* 9, second year of the Republic [July 27, 1794]) it was reduced to twelve judges and thirty members of the jury.

75. Rousselet, vol. I, pp. 147-48.

76. Ibid., vol. I, p. 155; Royer, pp. 242-43.

77. Ibid., vol. I, pp. 145-48; Royer, pp. 239-40.

78. On the *Directoire*, see Godechot, pp. 476-77; Rousselet, vol. I, pp. 154-55; Royer, pp. 242-44.

79. The oath was to maintain the constitution and to be faithful to the nation, to the law, and to the king (as long as he was not overthrown). Royer, p. 222.

80. Rousselet, vol. I, pp. 234-36.

81. Ibid., vol. I, p. 147.

82. Royer, p. 244.

Chapter 4

Popular Democracy and the Election of Judges in the United States

The question of why the United States departed so radically from Western traditions by choosing to elect judges is often raised. Several events affected the shift in the early nineteenth century from the British practice of appointing judges to the later American practice of popular election. The French Revolution of 1790 had profound effects in the United States, and notions of liberty and equality, which characterized that event, were translated on the American side of the Atlantic into calls for universal suffrage (of white males, at least) and accountability of all public officials. These concepts developed currency simultaneously with the fall from power of the Federalist party, a political party associated with an aristocratic view of political power. Federalists were replaced, at the national level, except in the judicial branch, by Jeffersonians who championed popular democracy. Reaction against elite notions of government and currents from the French Revolution combined to create a movement for expanded democracy in the United States.

One purely American phenomenon, the frontier movement in the West, also fueled a sense of individualism and equality. As Americans crossed the mountains and headed for the farther reaches of the continent, they became increasingly self-reliant and egalitarian, and it was largely these attributes that created a climate for the rise of Jacksonian democracy. This movement was one manifestation of a style of populism consistent with the basic American axiom of popular sovereignty. The results were dramatic enough to prompt Tocqueville to comment: "The people reign in the American political world as the Deity does in the Universe. They are the cause and the aim of all things; everything comes from them, and everything is absorbed in them."[1]

Judges were first elected for the lower courts in Georgia, beginning in 1812. Then Mississippi decided, in 1832, to elect all judges. From 1845 until 1958 every new state entering the union provided for an elected judiciary, and four of the original thirteen states changed to elections as the mode for designating judges.[2] These changes in state practices, however, were never seriously contemplated for the federal judiciary, which has remained appointive since the ratification of the Constitution. Nonetheless, events occurring at the national level were preludes to or catalysts for changes at the state level.

THE FRENCH REVOLUTION IN AMERICA

The French Revolution had important implications for the United States and, according to Parrington, altered the history of the United States as well as of France. Party issues and policies in America were often determined and limited by what was occurring on the other side of the Atlantic. Perhaps most importantly, the French Revolution made the term democracy reputable in the United States in a way that it had not been previously. Rather than being associated, as it had in post-revolutionary days, with anarchy and mob rule, the ideal of democracy became accepted as "the ultimate form of political organization" and the one to which America must aspire in its organization.[3]

The English declaration of war on France polarized parties and attitudes in the United States. The Federalist party supported Great Britain and was linked, therefore, to aristocratic beliefs and dogmas. The democrats, for the first time having a body of philosophy in their camp, became supporters of the French. Class alignments became sharp in the consciousness of the democrats as they began the move to eliminate vestiges of elitism from the American power system.[4]

Cleavages were sharp between the divergent approaches to government and could be traced in the writings of many of the pamphleteers of the times. Edmund Burke, in 1790, wrote his *Reflections on the Revolution in France* as an indictment of the French revolt and subsequent actions by the newly selected National Assembly. Many of Burke's sentiments were echoed on the other side of the Atlantic by John Adams, particularly in his *Discourses on Davila*. The rebuttal to both was Thomas Paine's *The Rights of Man*.

Burke was the only one of those writers who directly addressed the judicial system erected after the French Revolution, but the others considered the subject indirectly. Specifically, Burke assailed the procedure established for electing judges in France, first by lauding their earlier system for appointing jurists, a system he perceived to be akin to that used in Britain. Referring to the jurists under the French monarchy, Burke extolled them for "one fundamental excellence: they were independent."[5] He noted that judges under the French king were appointed for life, "indeed they may be said to have held by inheritance." "Appointed by the monarch," he continued, "they were considered as nearly out of his power."[6] Having this independence, the courts had been able to preserve the French constitution and secure private property.

Burke then attacked the new system of popular election of judges as least desirable once the country became a democracy:

> Elective, temporary, local judges, such as you have contrived, exercising the dependent functions in a narrow society, must be worst of all tribunals. In them it will be vain to look for any appearance of justice toward strangers, toward the obnoxious rich, toward the minority of routed parties, toward all those who in the election have supported unsuccessful candidates. It will be impossible to keep the new tribunals clear of the worst spirit of faction.[7]

And Burke's final indictment of this method for selecting judges exceeded issues of the courts and extended to all manner of elections. "All contrivances by ballot we know experimentally," he contended, "to be vain and childish and prevent a discovery of inclinations."[8]

The last remark of Burke is likely the most critical demarcation between those promoting English liberalism and those moved by French democratic theories. John Adams, in 1790, wrote an American version of the position voiced by Burke. Adams, too, was dismayed by the events in France in 1790. Writing about the French Revolution and encouraging Americans to avoid a similar fate, he argued that as knowledge becomes more widely disseminated, "it becomes the more indispensable that every man should know his place and be made to keep it", as "bad men increase in knowledge as fast as good men."[9]

Adams took offense at the excesses of the French Revolution, as he saw them, and, in particular, the absence of restraints on human nature and human passions: "Frenchmen! Act and think like yourselves! . . . Consider that government is intended to set bounds to passions which nature has not limited; and to assist reason, conscience, justice, and truth in controlling interests which without it would be as unjust as uncontrollable."[10] He then turned to the American situation. He urged his countrymen to benefit from their experiences with a well-ordered government. "Instead of following any foreign example," he urged, or returning "to the *legislation of confusion*, contemplate the means of restoring decency, honesty, and order in society by preserving and completing . . . the balance of your government."[11]

The basic tenets of Adams' arguments against the new French government were that distinctions between rich and poor were eliminated and private property was not secure. The base of all these problems was the controversy between those with and those without property. "But if unlimited or unbalanced power of disposing property be put into the hands of those who have no property," he admonished, "France will find, as we have found, the lamb committed to the custody of the wolf."[12] Thus Adams voiced the same concerns as Burke against the passions and leveling influences of the French Revolution. Both supported the brand of English liberalism that protected property and that recognized class distinctions. Their arguments denied that popular democracy, particularly extended to the point of making all officials accountable to the popular will (inclusive of judges) and without regard for property as a requirement for voting, could cause anything but confusion, anarchy, and an end to balanced government.

Thomas Paine, on the other hand, defended the French Revolution and the actions of the National Assembly in formulating the new French constitution. Paine was in France when he wrote *The Rights of Man* as a direct rebuttal to Burke. When it was printed in America the pamphlet carried a preface by Thomas Jefferson that asserted that its publication was essential to answer the "political heresies which have sprung up among us."[13] Later Andrew Jackson said that the book would be "more enduring than all the piles of marble and granite man can erect."[14] Indeed, as well as being a response to Burke, Paine's *The Rights of Man* provided a philosophical statement for democratic movements in America.

Paine's response to Burke's indictment of the elected judiciary in France was not direct. Rather, he dealt with basic issues of French democracy versus English liberalism and with basic ideas of popular election, without property requirements attached to the franchise. The French constitution based extension of the franchise on the payment of a tax each year. Thus what Paine perceived to be a type of universal suffrage was possible in France, in contrast to the "capricious" qualifications practiced in England at the time.[15] Further, all of these electors were able to participate in selection of the National Assembly, whose representatives were apportioned on the basis of taxable inhabitants.[16] Implicit in those provisions was that judges would be chosen by the same electors, not only by those with property. And from these comments the inference can be made that such judges would be superior to those "vicious judges" in England, whom he had earlier described as prosecuting as libel an admittedly true public statement.

> "The greater the truth, the greater the libel," is a legal maxim constantly applied by the judges, [and] it ought to be easy to satisfy the world that truth has always been suppressed in England. This insult to public morals has received the name of law, and there are vicious judges who actually sentence truth to punishment.[17]

The essential difference between Burke or Adams, on the one side, and Paine, on the other, revolved around who has the ability to exercise political power. Property holding and class distinctions were critical for both Burke and Adams. Paine contended, however, that

> sovereignty, as a matter of right, appertains to the nation only, and not to any individual; and a nation has at all times an inherent, indefeasible right to abolish and establish such as accords with its interests, disposition, and happiness. . . . Every citizen is a member of the sovereignty, and, as such, can acknowledge no personal subjection; and his obedience can be only to the laws.[18]

Thus, for the period of the 1790s, many of the lines were drawn for the confrontation to follow between republicanism and democracy in the United States and the corollaries of each position for the selection and tenure of judges in the American states.

Another strain of political thought, influenced by the French Revolution, was arising in the same period and would affect American political thought. That was found in the writings of the new British liberals—democrats in the English liberal tradition. They were known as philosophical radicals, of whom the utilitarians constituted the group that is most important for our consideration. Their writings were the result not of a political revolution, but of the industrial revolution. Utilitarianism was a philosophy of individualism, and one that would be adapted by those involved in the western expansion of the United States.

Jeremy Bentham, the foremost thinker of the utilitarians, shared that distrust of the judiciary that had motivated the French to choose judges through elections. Bentham thought that English judges and lawyers (he called them "Judge and Co.") worked against the public interest. Judges formed a class separate from the rest of society that did not identify with societal interests. The judges, Bentham alleged, created laws of procedure, designed to favor the judicial corporation at the expense of the public. Judge and Co., he contended, had as their goal the creation of a system of formalism that was obscure, long, and costly for the parties, but lucrative and easy for the collusive group of judges and barristers. This led Bentham to adopt the theme of "everyman, his own lawyer."[19] Thus Bentham and the philosophic radicals expressed contempt for those manning the British benches, who had been appointed by the Crown.

Reactions in America to the French Revolution and the responses of British liberals to the industrial revolution afforded an ideological framework for the inclinations that were beginning to emerge in the United States. The Federalist party, whose political thought is well represented by John Adams, remained in power until 1801. The last years of their governance was alleged to be abusive, or at least created a sense of insecurity in the country. The courts were not immune to the reactions that ultimately brought the demise of the Federalist party and that thrust the United States into a period in which populism was on the rise.

RISE OF JEFFERSONIAN DEMOCRACY

The rise of Jeffersonian democracy, under the guise of the Democratic-Republican party, was largely due to the excesses of the Federalist party during their last term in office. The Federalists had been quite successful in the congressional elections of 1798 and had managed to gain an overwhelming majority in Congress committed to their programs. Among the bills passed were the Alien and Sedition Acts, which their rivals, Republicans and Jeffersonians, labeled as violative of the freedom of speech. They also created an expectation of imminent war with France, which was detrimental to business, as men were in a state of limbo while waiting for the call to military service. The expense of the demonstration for war also took its toll on the Federalist cause, as 3.5 million dollars had to be borrowed by the federal government, at 8 percent interest. Adams grew to be an unpopular President, and George Washington, who had provided much credibility for the Federalists, died. There were reactions against the direct tax levied by Congress and against the inability of the government to protect American citizens against British impressment of seamen.[20]

Federalist judges were likewise culpable in bringing their party into disrepute. Moreover, these jurists' had, by the early nineteenth century, created sufficient ill will to lead some to ponder the necessity of judicial reform. The first U.S. judges had been appointed by President Washington, and he, by all accounts, made his selections with a degree of deliberate care. He described the difficulty of the task, as follows:

> No part of my duty will be more delicate, and in many instances, more unpleasing, than that of nominating or appointing persons to offices. It will undoubtedly often happen that there will be several candidates for the same offices whose pretensions, abilities and integrity may be nearly equal, and who will come forward equally supported in every respect, as almost to require the aid of supernatural intuition to fix upon the right. I shall, however, in all events, have the satisfaction to reflect that I entered upon my administration unconfined by a single engagement, uninfluenced by any ties of blood or friendship, and with the best intentions and fullest determination to nominate to office those persons only, who, upon every consideration, were the most deserving, and who would probably execute their several functions to the interest and credit of the American Union.[21]

The first thirteen individuals whom he nominated for the district courts in 1789 were described as "truly fit characters."[22] Washington's chagrin resulted from the declination of the position by some of his nominees. By the end of his term in office he had named fifty-one people to the federal judiciary and an additional fifty-five replacements owing to declinations, resignations, and deaths.[23] Despite the care that the first President had attempted in his nominations, there were some difficulties from the outset. The potential for conflict of interest or partisanship arose as thirteen of his appointees as U.S. judges, attorneys, and marshals continued to hold other offices, at either the state or the national level.[24]

Much criticism was laid at the feet of the federal judges, who were of the Federalist party, because of their handling of Alien and Sedition Act prosecutions. The most notorious of these was the Supreme Court justice Samuel Chase, whose behavior while riding circuit ultimately led to his impeachment by the House of Representatives. Chase was believed to have been overly zealous and partisan in his trying of crimes under the Sedition Act of 1798. In at least two cases, Justice Chase was so unduly difficult on the defense attorneys that they withdrew from the case, claiming that their clients could not receive fair trials.[25] He was also considered to be unabashedly partial to Federalists before his court and had a "cavalier approach toward the concept of impartial juries."[26] Although he was not impeached until 1804 (and ultimately acquitted by the Senate in 1805),[27] his activities and the publicity that they drew worked against the Federalist party in the election of 1800.

Justice Chase was not the only Federalist judge or prosecutor accused of exercising a form of tyranny in the execution of the Alien and Sedition Act. At least eighteen persons were charged with either publishing or making libelous statements, punishable under the act. Three of those who were convicted and fined under the law were inebriated Republicans who made vulgar, drunken remarks to one another about the proximity of a canon's trajectory to the backside of Federalist President Adams. Three others were convicted for publishing libelous articles. The largest fine was imposed on a U.S. representative from Vermont who simply criticized the national government. In all, of the eighteen charged between 1798 and 1800, one defendant died, prosecution was dropped in five cases, and eleven were convicted and received fines ranging from 5 dollars to 1,500 dollars and prison terms ranging from two to eighteen months. Only one person was acquitted in a trial before a federal judge.[28]

More than one Federalist judge was unduly hasty in trying allegations of treason under the Alien and Sedition Act. For example, in 1798 a group of men in Bethlehem, Pennsylvania, attacked a group of federal tax assessors and stole their assessment rolls. Twenty-three men were arrested. John Fries led a mob to forcibly remove those men arrested and not previously freed on parole. Once the mob was subdued, ninety-five were indicted, three for treason. One of these, Fries, was convicted, although he won a retrial on appeal because of the admitted prejudice of a juror. Unfortunately for Fries, his second trial, at which he was convicted and sentenced to death, was presided over by Justice Chase. Subsequently President Adams pardoned Fries and two others convicted of treason in the affair.[29]

Judges of the Federalist party on state benches were also responsible for creating a negative image of the judiciary. Judge Alexander Addison was impeached and convicted by the Pennsylvania legislature for making an anti-Republican political address to a grand jury, while prohibiting an associate judge of the rival party from making any comments to the same jury.[30] Another Pennsylvania judge, also a Federalist, cited one party in a civil case for contempt of court and sentenced him to thirty days in prison. The offense that merited this punishment was the party's refusal to apologize, on order of the judge, to the opposing party, whom he had called a liar, a rascal, and a coward.[31] Such events resulted in the following article in the Philadelphia *Aurora*:

> The frequent abuse of power by judges of the courts and justices of the peace will one day render a total revision of the received maxims concerning the tenure of judicial office necessary. It will one day be a subject of enquiry, why judges and justices of the peace should be more independent of the control of a free people, than those who have the formation and the execution of the laws entrusted to them. It will become a subject of enquiry, whether there is any analogy between what is called the *independence of the judges* in England, and the independence of the judges in America—and whether making the former independent of the *King* justified making the latter independent of the people.[32]

These events and others enabled the Republicans under Jefferson to come to power, although the Presidential election was thrown into the House of Representatives and required thirty-six ballots to name Jefferson over his Vice-Presidential running mate, Burr. Bassett concludes that the Federalist party lost because it was no longer in step with the country:

> Its function of giving strength to the Union in the early days of "the experiment" had been performed. It was the party of the superior classes, of men who were supposed not to be influenced by passions and who had strong purposes and conservative instincts. It had solved the problems of the effective organization of a new government; but other questions were now at hand concerning internal affairs.[33]

The Federalists had, in the closing days of their power, passed the Judiciary Act of 1801, which had the effect of placing the federal judicial system squarely into politics for the next generation. The purely partisan aspects of the Federalist plan can be clearly seen in Kentucky, where the district court with its single judge was replaced by a three-judge circuit court. Sitting district judges with Jeffersonian leanings were not promoted to the circuit bench; rather, novice Federalists were brought into the circuit positions. Even unexplained salary differentials were made to favor the new Federalist appointees over their predecessors, and the site of the court was moved to a town more convenient for the newly appointed judges, one of whom was the brother-in-law of Federalist Supreme Court Justice John Marshall. "These Federalist judiciary acts were further evidence of what they [Kentuckians] perceived to be inattention," explains Tauchau, "and even disregard by the federal government of the problems of the people beyond the mountains."[34]

The Federalists were replaced by a party reflective of current trends of thinking—emphasizing the will of the people. The tenets of the new breed of politicians are perhaps best captured in the first inaugural address of Thomas Jefferson. What he deemed to be the essential principles of the government were equal justice to all, respect for the powers of the state governments, preservation of the federal government, the right of election by the people, and acquiescence in majority rule. These, he said, are "the vital principles of republics."

Jeffersonian democracy represented several significant deviations from earlier Federalist conceptions. The general principles of government that Jefferson espoused also had an impact on his view, and that of his followers, of the proper role and place of the judiciary. Perhaps the most telling difference between the Jeffersonian view of government and that of the constitutional draftsmen is illustrated in their responses to Shays' Rebellion. The framers, you will recall, took that uprising as a signal to avoid popular democracy as the first step toward mob rule. Jefferson, on the other hand, in 1787, wrote to Madison that national reaction to the rebellion was excessive. "Calculate that one rebellion in thirteen states in the course of eleven years, is but one for each state in a century and a half," and he added, "no country should be so long without one."[35] He elaborated by saying that the reaction of seeking a stronger government would not be a barrier to other insurrections.

Two other basic elements of Jeffersonian thought, which would have implications for judicial selection and tenure, are his conceptions of the place of majority rule and the need for universal suffrage. He believed that majority rule was a primary tenet:

> To consider the will of the society enounced by the majority of a single vote, as sacred as if unanimous, is the first of all lessons in importance, yet the last which is thoroughly learnt. This law, once disregarded, no other remains but that of force, which ends necessarily in military despotism.[36]

And the corollary to majority rule was that the franchise should not be limited to those owning property. In a letter to J. Moor in 1800, Jefferson explained that although many viewed the property requirement as necessary to prevent the buying and selling of votes, his response was to make the "number of voters too great for any means of purchase." Property-holding would not lend greater voter independence as, "I have not observed men's honesty to increase with their riches."[37]

The twin concepts of majority rule and universal suffrage, during the subsequent period of Jacksonian democracy, were directly tied to the desire to have an elective judiciary. Jefferson himself had wavered in his attitude toward selection of persons for the bench. He had consistently contended that the judiciary was the branch of the national government that was "anti-Republican" because judicial officers held their position for life.[38] The judges were "self-appointed, self-continued, holding their authorities for life," and therefore, he observed, the people were incapable of "breaking in on the perpetual succession of any faction once possessed of the bench."[39]

Jefferson had originally believed that judges should hold their offices for life, so that their independence could be guaranteed. In 1776 he had written to Wythe that the nation's jurists should be insulated from "jarring interests" and should not be "dependent upon any man or body of men."[40] By 1789 he had become convinced that although permanent judges might develop some biases that would be injected into their decisions, the jury was the great counter to corruption of judges.[41] However, after frustrating encounters with the Supreme Court under John Marshall, he altered his opinion. He asserted that the Court under Marshall had made the Constitution "a mere thing of wax in the hands of the judiciary."[42] Once appointed, the judges were unassailable, for "the impeachment it [the Constitution] has provided is not even a scarecrow."[43] He came to view the federal judiciary as no more than "the subtle corps of sappers and miners" attempting to undermine the principles of government.[44]

A consequence of Jefferson's disillusionment with so independent a judiciary was his consideration of other means of selecting or removing judges. One of his recommendations was a federal judiciary with terms of six years, to be reappointed only on approval of the executive and both houses of Congress.[45] He also proposed that judges should be popularly elected, although his full enthusiasm for the prospect was not apparent in his letters:

> It has been thought that the people are not competent electors of judges *learned in the law*. But I do not know that this is true, and, if doubtful, we should follow principle. In this, as in many other elections, they would be guided by reputation, which would not err oftener, perhaps, than the present mode of appointment. In one State of the Union, at least, it has long been tried and with the most satisfactory success. . . . I believe there has hardly ever been an instance of change; so powerful is the curb of incessant responsibility.[46]

Factors other than national partisan positions affected changes in perceptions of the proper role of the judiciary and of who should name people to exercise the judicial role. Debates in the states often followed several themes; among them were issues of the political monopoly of the legal profession and the lack of attractiveness of judicial positions. The arguments were often between factional alliances within parties as well as between parties. Gawalt, in his study of the use of the legal profession in Massachusetts, notes the rise of the "lawyer politician," which promoted an anti-lawyer sentiment. Local bar associations had been formed in the 1790s to police qualifications for those at the bar and to establish minimum fee structures. Indeed, "the interdependence and mutual assistance of the judiciary and the legal profession," he suggested, "was a well-established political and economic fact."[47] A collaboration akin to Bentham's "Judge and Co." was a reality in post-revolutionary Massachusetts, and there was an attempt by the two cooperating bodies to limit competition.

Jeffersonian Republicans chose to capitalize on the anti-lawyer sentiments that resulted from increased fees charged for legal services and from the disproportionate number of lawyers holding governmental positions. Yet lawyers holding political offices were as likely to be Jeffersonians as Federalists, as they, "like other politicians, reflected their constituencies."[48] Even so, there existed a concern that one profession could dominate two branches of government, the legislative and the judicial. Some Massachusetts Jeffersonians, therefore, pushed removal of lawyers from the ranks of the judiciary by allowing the governor to make appointments as part of general judicial reform until 1840.[49]

A portion of this paradox can be explained in that the Jeffersonians, like other political parties, were not homogenous in their attitudes toward the judiciary. Further, issues surrounding courts were different at the state level than at the national level. However, two themes tended to dominate discussions of judicial reform among Republicans: the insulation of the judiciary from public accountability because of life tenure and the relationship of the legislative to the judicial branch.[50] Impeachment had not proved to be a viable means of drawing federal jurists into account, which had exacerbated the sense of legislative impotence *vis-à-vis* the judiciary at the national level.

Federalist control of the federal bench, which was regarded by many as oppressive, and early decisions of the Supreme Court under the leadership of Chief Justice Marshall, himself a Federalist, were the motivations of Jeffersonians to contemplate an alternative means of staffing the courts. Ellis contends that politics clearly were the dominant force behind actions of the federal courts in the early years of the Republic.[51] Indeed, Charles Warren catalogues battles between the U.S. Supreme Court and at least five states between 1809 and 1825. The disputes of Pennsylvania, Georgia, Virginia, Kentucky, and Maryland with the Court resulted from specific issues (e.g., the ability of Congress to incorporate a bank). The underlying theme in these conflicts, however, was that initially enunciated by the anti-federalists in ratification debates—national judicial encroachment on the rights of the states.[52] Discontent with the national judiciary led many, such as Jefferson, to look for alternative means for determining its composition. And the French Revolution, with its emphasis on egalitarianism and accountability of public officials, offered an example to emulate. The radical change in how judges were designated, however, was to occur later, in the context of the larger movement of Jacksonian democracy.

JACKSONIAN DEMOCRACY

The United States underwent a period of readjustment after the War of 1812, a process that lasted until the election of Andrew Jackson as President in 1829. The period preceding Jackson's election was one in which sectional interests and national interests clashed and in which Western frontiers were extended. Jacksonian democracy characterizes a period extending from Jackson's election until either the end of his tenure in office in 1837 or, according to some, until the advent of the Civil War. The phrase Jacksonian democracy has become a shorthand statement for experiments in democracy—"the extensions of the franchise, the attacks on privilege and deference, [and] the swelling spirit of popular rule."[53] By all accounts this constituted a major new era in American politics, an era of "self-conscious American democracy."[54]

The emigration to and development of the frontier in America created a climate in which reconsideration of the fundamentals of government was nurtured. Parrington calls the frontiersmen "coonskin individualists" who took Jeffersonian thought seriously and who truly believed in equality because it comported with their experiences. Democracy was the faith of the West.[55] Constitutions enacted by the new states entering the Union after 1812 all exhibit some characteristics attributable to the Western sense of democracy. With the exception of Mississippi, the new Western constitutions provided for universal male suffrage. Likewise, legislatures for the new states were apportioned on the basis of white population. The latter was, according to Turner, indicative that the prevailing doctrine was the "rule of the majority rather than that of property."[56]

The driving force behind the new democracy in the West was class consciousness, "the will to destroy the aristocratic principle in government."[57] "Rule by the few, the well-educated or well-born" was to be replaced by egalitarianism.[58] According to Blau, however, the classes involved in the new struggle were two divisions of the middle class, one that was Federalist and composed of capitalists and financiers. The lower middle class, which was the proponent of the new democracy, consisted of farmers, landowners, artisans, and mechanics. And there was the new working class of industrial laborers in the Eastern urban centers. These groups, joined loosely together in a rather motley aggregation, advocated universal suffrage, the end of privilege, and an end to imprisonment for debt.[59] The reorganization of American life that occurred as a consequence was social, political, and economic and constituted a clear break with tradition.[60]

Andrew Jackson was the hero of the frontiersmen and of those growing classes of industrial workers in the Eastern cities. "Democracy came to its own when Andrew Jackson triumphed over the old order of things" and, according to Turner, "rudely threw open the sanctuary of federal government to the populace."[61] Jackson was not concerned with social or political philosophy; he acted on the basis of integrity, realism, and plain fact.[62] As a result, others devised the political theories that are associated with his name and his actions. Perhaps the clearest statements of Jacksonian democracy are found in the introduction to the first issue of *The United States Magazine and Democratic Review* in 1837, whose stated purpose was advocacy of "that high and holy *democratic principle*." The first principle was self-government and democratic republicanism because of confidence in the "full capacity for self-government, of the great mass of our people, our . . . intelligent millions of freemen."[63] Self-government translated into, among other things, the movement for universal male suffrage. The second basic element of democratic republicanism was minimal government, the government "which governs least."[64] And finally, democracy meant freedom or the voluntary principle.[65]

Jackson was not viewed as a supporter of the federal judiciary and definitely not a champion of Chief Justice John Marshall. Frederick Robinson, in a speech delivered to the Trades' Union of Boston and Vicinity, in 1834, probably encapsulates the extreme Jacksonian view of the judiciary. "The judiciary in this State, and in every State where judges hold their office during life," he contended, "is the headquarters of the aristocracy."[66] To Robinson, judges were placed alongside such undesirables as capitalists, monopolists, lawyers, and priests.[67] Judges, in combination with lawyers, constituted an evil that should be contained. Robinson explained how to approach judicial reform.

> In the first place, judges should be made responsible to the people by periodical elections. The boast of an independent judiciary is always made to deceive you. We want no part of our government independent of the people. Those who are responsible to nobody ought to be entrusted by nobody. But to whom are the judges responsible? The aristocracy always center around power placed beyond the reach of the people.[68]

Robinson's position and that of the Jacksonians never altered the federal judiciary, but did influence expectations placed on the state judiciaries.[69]

Some contend that the sentiment for popular election of judges was a direct consequence of Jacksonian democracy. Others, in particular Kermit Hall, dispute that. He explains:

> The rise of popular, partisan election of appellate judges is best understood as an essentially thoughtful response by constitutionally moderate lawyers and judges in the Whig, Democratic, and Republican parties. . . . Lawyers and judges—not wild-eyed agrarian and urban radicals—controlled the all-important committees on the judiciary in the state constitutional conventions that adopted popular election.[70]

Members of the legal profession supported popular election as a means of guaranteeing the independence of the judiciary by providing that branch of government with its own base of legitimacy.[71] Regardless of the specific motivations of those drafting the amendments that altered how judicial officers were to be named, popular election of judges became vogue coterminously with Jacksonian democracy.

In 1832 Mississippi wrote a new constitution designed to be more democratic than that of 1817. And that constitution was the first in the United States to provide that all judges would serve for specific terms and be named through popular election. This action in Mississippi was the result of a general trend for greater democracy, but it was largely a direct response to specific problems in the Mississippi judiciary that had defied remedial action under the previous constitutional mechanisms. Three consecutive Mississippi legislatures had attempted unsuccessfully to impeach one supreme court justice, Joshua Child. Child had been charged with dueling, drunkenness, and official misconduct. Perhaps his greatest crime, though, was declaring an act of the Mississippi legislature unconstitutional in the case of *Cochrane v. Kitchens* in 1824. Frustration at the impossibility of removing a judge through the impeachment process was the primary catalyst for the change to popular election.[72]

The problem of legislative removal of judges was not uncommon in the early nineteenth century. Indeed, Howard notes the issue as part of the ongoing debate in Virginia, where in 1816 Jefferson had complained that judges were responsible to no one. Marshall, in an address to the Virginia constitutional convention of 1829–30, had championed the opposing position, that a judge should be controlled by no others, save God and his own conscience. Virginia's 1830 constitution provided for election of judges by vote of the legislative assembly and, likewise, their removal by vote of that same assembly "for any reason they think proper to assign."[73]

Kentucky confronted the question of removing undesirable judges in 1823 and created a novel approach. The Kentucky court of appeal had evoked the displeasure of the legislature by striking down laws providing for debt relief. As two-thirds majority required for impeachment was not attainable, the disgruntled legislature abolished the court completely. An entirely new court, with judges appointed by the governor, was established.[74] The difficulty of impeaching judges was, in more than one state, a primary motive for following the lead of Mississippi and changing both the mode of removal and the means of selection.

As no state constitution was a pure innovation, once one state formulated a new means of coping with a common problem, others were likely to adopt some version of the system. In addition to simple borrowing from one state to another, new states either appropriated language from neighboring states or the prior states of many settlers. Often new states tended to accept the most recently conceived approaches.[75] Therefore, that eighteen additional states, between 1832 and 1861, adopted popular election of judges with set terms of office is in keeping with natural proclivities of constitutional draftsmen.

Popular election of judges was not the only change to be found in state constitutions, which was connected with Jacksonian democracy. Universal manhood suffrage, without property requirements, was introduced. Apportionment plans that were population-based were also common in the new state constitutions. Most elements of the Jacksonian democratic reforms, such as the extension of the franchise, have been retained or even expanded over the ensuing century. Indeed, some have proposed that this era established "the fundamental practices and patterns of the future."[76] Little criticism has been directed at greater democratization of most elements of political life. The influence of this populist period on the judicial system has, however, drawn massive criticism, particularly in the twentieth century. The controversy begun in the first half of the nineteenth century over the selection and tenure of judges in the American states has not yet abated.

DEMOCRACY AND THE JUDICIARY

The process of electing judges in the American states remains an innovation in the whole of the Western world. This American experiment truly constitutes a break with all of the European traditions that came to America with its early inhabitants. Whereas the outcome of a process begun shortly after the ratification of the U.S. Constitution seems incongruous to others, the election of judges was a natural outgrowth of the American experience in the early nineteenth century.

Two sets of events led the American public to distrust and question the post-revolutionary schemes governing selection and tenure of judges. The French Revolution, with its emphasis on democratic government, directly affected American thinking about political power and the meaning of popular sovereignty. Distrust of a judiciary responsible to no person or group was a natural extension of a re-evaluation of the arrangement of political power in government. Thomas Paine's *The Rights of Man* was the dramatic American statement of the desirability of French democracy in lieu of British liberalism.

The French Revolution and its notions about political power might have had only a passing influence on American politics had it not occurred in juxtaposition with allegedly abusive, anti-democratic actions by the Federalist government during its last two years in office. The Federalists were perceived as the heirs of British liberalism, as protectors of a privileged aristocracy. The demise of that party in 1801 was the result of discontent with limited, class-based political participation. Jefferson and the Republicans replaced the Federalists, except initially in the judicial branch, and began to articulate Americanized visions of democracy, popular sovereignty, and French revolutionary ideals.

The Jeffersonians laid the groundwork for a stronger democracy, but the rise of the frontier in the West and the election of the frontiersman's hero to the Presidency created the circumstances for dramatic changes in government. Jacksonian democracy espoused universal manhood suffrage, accountability of political officials, and representation based on population. Its purported aim was to remove vestiges of elitism in government. Much of what Jacksonian democracy accomplished and represented might never have received political currency had there not been a rise of economic individualism in the West and the development of a new middle class, which could be mobilized along with the new industrial working class of the Eastern cities. Merger of the interests of these groups facilitated a momentum for the new American democratic ideals.

There are several ironies in how these ideals of the Jeffersonians worked in reality. One is that actions of the federal judiciary, and, in particular, the U.S. Supreme Court under Marshall, constituted one spark for Jeffersonian and Jacksonian opposition to judges who were decidedly independent. Yet the selection system, tenure, and removal mechanisms for the federal judiciary remained intact throughout the populist era and subsequently.

A second unanticipated consequence of this movement was that a class of people antithetical to the goals of popular democracy was named to the federal courts in this era. A basic tenet of Jacksonian democracy was the elimination of privilege. Yet, as John Schmidhauser has demonstrated, the Supreme Court has, in all historical periods, been staffed by people of upper-middle-class or elite origins.[77] Kermit Hall analyzed the 101 judges on the federal courts from 1829 to 1861 and found that only one-fifth of these jurists came from humble origins; the backgrounds of the judges were predominantly elite or well-to-do. They were nine-tenths of British origins and had been intensely active in elective politics.[78] Thus, despite some small carry-over from the Federalist regime, those who were named to the bench by Presidents advocating popular democracy did not violate the tradition of privilege among federal jurists.

Also, Jefferson and his successors left a mark on the judiciary, both federal and state, that they might not have realized. Friedman contends that the unsuccessful attempts at impeachment may have been battles lost, but wars won. The threat of impeachment was sufficient to curb overtly partisan actions by federal judges.

> The judges won independence, but at a price. Their openly political role was reduced; and ultimately, most states turned to the elective principle. There would be no more impeachments, but also no more Chases. What carried the day, in a sense, was the John Marshall solution. The judges would take refuge in professional decorum. . . . Justice would be blind; and it would wear a poker face.[79]

The institution of an elected judiciary at the state level forestalled further attempts at partisan-motivated impeachments, as such were no longer necessary.

No reaction against the elective system was seriously considered until 1906, when Roscoe Pound, in an address to the American Bar Association, issued his scathing indictment of the caliber and reputation of the elected bench in the United States.[80] Since that time, attacks on the system for electing judges have been frequent, forceful, and common. The result, which is discussed in greater depth in Chapter 6, has been creation of myriad schemes for selecting judges in the American states—processes that attempt to preserve aspects of the appointive systems and the accountability of elective systems. Variations are extensive, such that no two states designate all judges in the same manner.[81] The legacy of Jacksonian democracy continues to thrive through the election of judges in many American states. Elections have, however, not yielded results either so good or so bad as expected by their advocates or detractors.[82]

NOTES

1. Alexis de Tocqueville, *Democracy in America*, ed. Phillips Bradley (New York: Vintage Books, 1954), p. 260.
2. Glenn R. Winters, "Selection of Judges—An Historical Introduction," 44 *Texas Law Review* (1966), p. 1081.
3. Vernon Louis Parrington, *Main Currents in American Thought* (New York: Harcourt, Brace, & World, 1927), vol. I, pp. 327–28.
4. Ibid., vol. I, pp. 328–29.
5. Edmund Burke, *Reflections on the Revolution in France*, ed. Thomas H. D. Mahoney (New York: Liberal Arts Press, 1955), p. 242.
6. Ibid.
7. Ibid., p. 243.
8. Ibid.
9. John Adams, *The Political Writings of John Adams*, ed. George A. Peek, Jr. (New York: Liberal Arts Press, 1954), p. 189.
10. Ibid., pp. 190–91.
11. Ibid., p. 191.
12. Ibid., p. 193.
13. Philip S. Foner, ed., *The Life and Major Writings of Thomas Paine* (Secaucus, N.J.: Citadel Press, 1948), p. 243.
14. Ibid.
15. Ibid., p. 280.
16. Ibid., p. 294.
17. Ibid., p. 248.
18. Ibid., p. 341.
19. Elie Halevy, *The Growth of Philosophic Radicalism* (Boston: Beacon Press, 1966), pp. 377–78.
20. John Spencer Bassett, *The Federalist System, 1789–1801* (New York: Harper & Brothers, 1906), pp. 277, 283.

21. Dwight F. Henderson, *Courts for a New Nation* (Washington, D.C.: Public Affairs Press, 1971), pp. 27–28.

22. Ibid., p. 28.

23. Ibid., p. 30.

24. Ibid., p. 29.

25. Bassett, pp. 284–85.

26. Henry J. Abraham, *The Judicial Process* (New York: Oxford University Press, 1980), p. 46.

27. The group attempting to remove Chase "overplayed its hand" and allowed overt partisanism to become a primary factor. Chase was acquitted, by a slim margin, largely because of defections from Jefferson's party. Lawrence M. Friedman, *A History of American Law* (New York: Simon & Schuster, 1973), pp. 114–15.

28. Henderson, pp. 124–27.

29. Ibid., pp. 126–32.

30. Richard E. Ellis, *The Jeffersonian Crisis: Courts and Politics in the Young Republic* (New York: Oxford University Press, 1971), pp. 164–65.

31. Ibid., pp. 165–66.

32. Ibid., p. 167.

33. Bassett, p. 295.

34. Mary K. Bonsteel Tachau, *Federal Courts in the Early Republic: Kentucky, 1789–1816* (Princeton, N.J.: Princeton University Press, 1978), p. 23.

35. Thomas Jefferson, *On Democracy*, ed. Saul K. Padover (New York: Mentor Books, 1939), p. 23.

36. Ibid., p. 34.

37. Ibid., p. 38.

38. Ibid., p. 40.

39. Ibid., pp. 40–41.

40. Ibid., p. 61.

41. Ibid., p. 62.

42. Merrill D. Peterson, ed., *The Portable Thomas Jefferson* (Harmondsworth: Penguin Press, 1977), p. 563.

43. Ibid., p. 562.

44. Jefferson, *On Democracy*, p. 63.

45. Ibid., p. 65.

46. Ibid., pp. 62–63.

47. Gerard W. Gawalt, *The Promise of Power: The Emergence of the Legal Profession in Massachusetts, 1760–1840* (Westport, Conn.: Greenwood Press, 1979), p. 91.

48. Ibid., p. 95.

49. Ibid., p. 99.

50. Ellis, pp. 233–34.

51. Ibid., p. 7.

52. Charles Warren, *The Supreme Court in United States History, 1789–1918* (Boston: Little, Brown, & Co., 1926), vol. I, pp. 366–633.

53. Robert V. Remini, *The Revolutionary Age of Andrew Jackson* (New York: Harper & Row, 1976), p. 69.

54. Frederick Jackson Turner, *Rise of the New West, 1819–1829* (New York: Harper & Brothers, 1906), p. 9.

55. Parrington, vol. II, pp. 137–38.

56. Turner, p. 175.

57. Parrington, vol. II, p. 145.

58. Remini, p. 178.

59. Joseph L. Blau, ed., *Social Theories of Jacksonian Democracy* (New York: Liberal Arts Press, 1947), p. xiv.

60. William McDonald, *Jacksonian Democracy, 1829–1837* (New York: Harper & Brothers, 1906), pp. 3–4.

61. Turner, p. 9.

62. Parrington, vol. II, pp. 146–47.

63. Blau, p. 22.

64. Ibid., p. 27.

65. Ibid., p. 28.

66. Ibid., p. 328.

67. Ibid., p. 330.

68. Ibid., p. 332.

69. Despite the general perception of Jackson as anti-Supreme Court, his stirring response to the 1832 South Carolina Ordinance of Nullification was highly supportive of the national courts. Indeed, some have interpreted that address as indicating that Jackson "embraced the constitutional principles of John Marshall." See Page Smith, *The Constitution: A Documentary and Narrative History* (New York: William Morrow & Co. 1978), pp. 395–402.

70. Kermit Hall, "Progressive Reform and the Decline of Democratic Accountability: The Popular Election of State Supreme Court Judges, 1850–1920," 1984 *American Bar Foundation Research Journal (1984)*, pp. 347–48.

71. Ibid., p. 48.

72. Arlen B. Coyle, "Judicial Selection and Tenure in Mississippi," 43 *Mississippi Law Journal* (1972), p. 90.

73. A. E. Dick Howard, *Commentaries on the Constitution of Virginia* (Charlottesville: University of Virginia Press, 1974), vol. II, pp. 695–97.

74. Of interest is the fact that the "old court" refused to relinquish its authority. Eventually, after a period in which there were two courts of

appeal, the "old court" gained the legislative majority. Thus the "old court" was re-established and its judges were awarded back salaries. Friedman, p. 115.

75. Ibid., p. 108.

76. Remini, p. 178.

77. John R. Schmidhauser, "Justices of the Supreme Court: A Collective Portrait," 3 *Midwest Journal of Political Science* (February 1959), pp. 6–13.

78. Kermit L. Hall, "Social Backgrounds and Judicial Recruitment: A Nineteenth-Century Perspective on the Lower Federal Judiciary," 29 *Western Political Quarterly* (June 1976), pp. 246–51.

79. Friedman, p. 116.

80. Roscoe Pound, "The Causes of Popular Dissatisfaction with the Administration of Justice," reprinted in 20 *Journal of the American Judicature Society* (1937), p. 178.

81. Larry Berkson, Scott Beller, and Michele Grimaldi, *Judicial Selection in the United States: A Compendium of Provisions* (Chicago: American Judicature Society, 1981), p. 6.

82. Friedman, p. 323.

Chapter 5

Evolution of French Judges as Civil Servants

Napoleon Bonaparte assumed power on *brumaire* 18, eighth year of the Republic (November 9, 1799), and immediately concluded that France required a new constitution. The constitutional draftsmen were not inspired by philosophical doctrines, but rather were realists who wanted to profit from the rich experience of the past ten years. The constitution that was completed on *frimaire* 22, eighth year of the Republic (December 13, 1799), considered many elements, among them the system of justice. Bonaparte had a personal interest in the judiciary, which he wished to be strong, well informed, and conscious of its duties. Privileges were to be granted as compensation to jurists. Further, Bonaparte wanted to be viewed as a man of conciliation among a people who had been divided by the Revolution, and he was, therefore, a man of synthesis. From the *Ancien Régime* he retained the courts of appeal in civil procedure and the principle of *cassation*. From the revolutionary legislation he maintained arbitration, conciliation, justices of the peace, juries of judgment in criminal procedures,[1] and a logical hierarchy of judicial institutions. In other respects he was totally innovative.

The reform introduced by the constitution of the eighth year of the Republic was supplemented by two laws of *ventôse* 27, eighth year of the Republic (March 18, 1800). The system thereby established was almost definitive and remains the basis of the contemporary French judiciary. Naturally some modifications were made during the nineteenth and twentieth centuries, but none were fundamental. The system's endurance is undoubtedly the best test of its value. To analyze the statute of the judiciary from 1799 to the

1950s (before the 1958 constitution of the Fifth Republic), questions of judicial recruitment, careers, and relationships with the executive power should be considered.

JUDICIAL RECRUITMENT

The constitution of 1799, a speedily written document, included a completely new principle for recruiting judges, one having no link with the *Ancien Régime* or with the Revolution. On the contrary the qualities required of judges were difficult to define and demanded time to enunciate. The principle of appointment by the executive power was instituted in the constitution of 1799 and has been retained, despite frequent discussions, to the present time.

Near the end of the Revolution, you may recall, particularly during the *Directoire*, the system of election was not always respected and the government often made appointments. When the constitution of 1799 was written, one of its main authors, Sièyes, was absolutely against electoral systems in any domain, administrative as well as judicial.[2] Sièyes explained that in 1789, elections had been introduced as a means for the citizens to manifest their distrust of the executive power, but this need no longer existed. Bonaparte had reintroduced confidence in the institutions of government. And thus the system of elections was rejected, with the exception of justices of the peace, who continued to be elected until the tenth year of the Republic.[3] At that time, appointment by the executive power was consecrated.

The system introduced by Bonaparte was rather complex.[4] The *premier consul* appointed judges from candidates on lists of notables. There were three categories of lists, which can be visualized as a pyramid. At the base were all citizens of twenty-one years of age, who voted for candidates for public functions. One-tenth of these citizens constituted the lists of notables of the *communes*,[5] from whom were chosen the judges of first instance (*tribunaux de première instance*). Men on the lists of notables of the *communes* designated one-tenth of their number to the lists of notables for the departments, from whom were chosen the judges of appeal. In their turn those on the list of notables of the departments selected another one-tenth to form the national list of notables, from whom the senate chose judges of the *tribunal de cassation*. This system did not fully satisfy Bonaparte, who reformed it in the *sénatus-consulte* of *thermidor* 16, tenth year of the Republic (August 3, 1802). In effect, he passed a new constitution.[6] The lists of notables were replaced by electoral colleges. The colleges played an important role in naming people to administrative and political offices but had no effect on the judiciary. Evidently Napoleon preferred to appoint judges directly. In the royal ordinance of February 15, 1815, appointment for all judges was made the exclusive prerogative of the king.

Judges, as a result, were men of the executive branch. Later we will explain how they became professionals in the same sense as the judges of the *Ancien Régime*. Under the new system the question of whether or not judges could co-opt their future colleagues, as they had before the Revolution, was critical. Members of the Prosecution Department usually asked for information on the candidates, as could a president of a jurisdiction. In 1839 the first president of the court of appeal of Besancçn explained to the minister of justice that the criteria he followed were that the candidate must not belong to a family whose ambition was to earn money or whose father had held an office in the police department. Notably, during most of the nineteenth century, there was a preference for sons of the grand judicial families,[7] whereas at the end of that century and during the twentieth century, the social recruitment of jurists evolved into a quite different situation. In the latter era, judges were primarily sons of civil servants. This shift democratized considerably the judiciary and assimilated the judges with the civil servants in general.[8]

When the executive appointed a judge, he was always careful to respect rules regarding the number of magistrates required to make a decision. Therefore, there had to be three judges in the *tribunaux de première instance*, seven in appeal (only five in correctional affairs since the reform of 1810 and in civil affairs since the law of August 30, 1883), and eleven in the *tribunal de cassation*. In the important jurisdictions there were several sections, which multiplied even further the number of judges.[9] Since the Monarchy of July, statesmen criticized the excessive number of jurisdictions and judges.[10] Judges often had few cases to consider; their resulting idleness was not viewed as consistent with their dignity. Nevertheless, abolishing tribunals would have been an unpopular measure and would have been perceived as contrary to local interests. The system, consequently, remained unchanged until the law of August 30, 1883, which eliminated many judgeships but did not affect existing jurisdictions *per se*. The law of April 28, 1919, accomplished a similar reform, although the objective was not the reorganization of the judiciary. The aim of that law was to increase judicial salaries, without weighing too heavily on the state budget! In 1926 the financial situation of France was so precarious that *président du conseil* (prime minister) Poincaré, using his plenary powers, reduced the number of jurisdictions through his decree law (*décret-loi*) of September 3. This decree law provided for only one jurisdiction in each department. This was the first change in judicial organization since 1799. Reactions were immediate, as those judges who were transferred were plainly irritated and local merchants who "lost" a jurisdiction were more than discontented. The situation was so tense that the law of July 16, 1930, was enacted to revoke part of the reform. The decree law of March 28, 1934, was an innovation, in that it provided for one judge only in the small tribunals. On days when court was in session, neighboring judges were required to come, so as to attain the necessary number. This was a concrete application of the theory of itinerant judges that had been developed during the *Constituante*. This provision was more important than it first appeared and must be viewed in the general debate on the solo judge.[11] Since the beginning of the twentieth century several jurists have been favorable to the notion. The principle benefit was seen as an affirmation that a judge acting alone would assume a greater responsibility for his decision. In 1926 a proposal was submitted to the senate but not even discussed. Finally the decree law of 1934, albeit in a limited field, was implemented. Only near the end of World War II was the idea of a single judge, deciding cases alone, again considered. At the Liberation, special jurisdictions were created to judge all acts of collaboration with the enemy. As a result there were insufficient judges to staff the ordinary tribunals. The ordinance of January 13, 1945, allowed the *tribunaux de première instance* to make decisions with only one judge. This ordinance was far from enthusiastically accepted because litigants knew how the judge had decided. There was no longer the anonymity of a collegial decision, and the judge was tempted to temper his judgment. Another objection to the system of solo decision-making was that a young judge would not be initiated by his elderly colleagues while sitting alone. These complaints partly explain the abrogation of the ordinance by the law of August 18, 1948. Whereas the reform of 1934 had been one possible remedy for the excessive number of judges, another possibility was to diminish the number through less radical measures. The latter was more easily realized. The decree law of June 25, 1934, decided that only three magistrates were required in the courts of appeal; the law of July 23, 1947, reduced to nine the number of judges required for the *cour de cassation.*[12]

The principles affirmed throughout the nineteenth and twentieth centuries recognized clearly that the executive power was master in recruiting the judiciary. The executive felt this prerogative so acutely that he did not hesitate to appoint lay-persons, very often lawyers, directly to the highest offices of the magistrature as a reward for their political dispositions. Such a practice was consistently observed after each revolution of the nineteenth century.[13] This practice might be regarded as the precedent for the modern mode of recruitment of high civil servants directly from the outside (*recrutement au tour extérieur*). Generally speaking, appointment by the executive was not accepted universally, and a certain nostalgia for past systems would surface.

Some magistrates regretted the system of the *Ancien Régime*, conferring great independence to face the king and characterized by venality and hereditary transmission of offices. They tried to restore more or less officiously similar practices. During the Restoration and the Monarchy of July, there was no upper limit on age, such that judges could remain in office until their death (which they generally did). When a judge resigned he fully intended to designate his successor. Often he would name his son, although not always. The executive power was not hostile to this practice, so long as a judge did not receive any financial compensation that could be interpreted as a reappearance of the venality. To enforce this criterion, the chancellery was vigilant in investigating possible sales of judicial offices, despite the difficulty in detecting such contracts. Nevertheless the practice was apparently sufficiently prevalent to warrant a note, dated April 27, 1822, forbidding all pecuniary transactions concerning judicial offices. This prohibition was not strictly respected, and examples of violations can be found in

1831, 1842, and 1844. Yet, over time, sales of offices were less numerous, and whenever the chancellery discovered such an arrangement, it blocked the appointment of the beneficiary, rendering the contract ineffective. On the contrary the chancellery was often quite indulgent when a judge resigned in favor of his son. This practice persisted even after the decree of 1852, which set an age limit. The facts prove a sort of survival of hereditary transmission, as in the *Ancien Régime*. Examples of hereditary transmission can be found until 1912.[14] These dealings are interesting as a reminder that a new law—even a constitution—cannot easily change attitudes and mentalities formed over centuries.

The movement for elections developed for other reasons entirely. The principle of electing judges was regarded as a republican theme and regularly surfaced during the nineteenth century.[15] Its re-establishment was discussed first in 1848, during the provisional government (although without much hope of success), and later between 1880 and 1883. In the latter period the debates were vehement, probably because of the general context. Several anticlerical laws had been passed that judges tried to resist. The politicians felt that elected judges would have more republican sentiments and would be less resistant. In 1882 newly elected deputies took their seats in the Chamber of Deputies. Because they had based part of their campaign on reintroduction of the principle of electing judges, they proposed a vote. The principle was adopted by a margin of 275 to 208 votes. A commission was charged with writing the implementing legislation. Meanwhile a member of the Prosecution Department of the *Cour de Cassation* published a small booklet criticizing the system.[16] How was it possible to assure the independence of an elected judge? The candidates would be either the worst lawyers (i.e., those who had no cases) or simple adventurers. He acknowledged that the system was practiced in other countries but concluded that it was not viable in France. On June 2, 1882, the minister of justice addressed the parliament and contended that the American system had been a disaster. He provoked considerable laughter when he claimed that in some U.S. towns, thieves allegedly managed to have their accomplices elected. The proposal was again discussed in the Chamber of Deputies in January 1883. Clémenceau spoke in favor of elections as a reflection of republican and democratic ideals. Roche opposed the idea because of the experience of the Revolution, during which there were difficult relations between the judges and the governmental institutions of the Convention and the *Directoire*. A similar point was developed by Waldeck-Rousseau, who feared the rise of a judicial power. Finally, the law on elections was rejected by 274 to 224 votes.

These nostalgic manifestations marked the legislative attempts and debates on the best means to select judges. The quest for good judges occurred not only on issues of selection, but also on questions of personal qualities and requirements.

The Revolution removed a number of prejudices about who was qualified for judgeships. Religious convictions no longer mattered, and unfrocked priests even became judges during the First Empire. Protestants were appointed throughout the nineteenth century. The hostility against an illegitimate child was progressively neutralized. The practice of recruiting foreign judges continued through the First and Second empires.

Many of the post-revolutionary requirements were set forth in an administrative note of March 2, 1809. That note stated that candidates for judicial positions must be in good physical condition. The phrase was sufficiently vague to raise the issue of whether a blind person could be accepted; the Monarchy of July answered affirmatively. Interestingly, there had never been a question of accepting deaf people. Today prospective magistrates must, like other civil servants, pass a medical examination. As to moral conditions, the note of March 2 provided that candidates must enjoy civil and political rights, behave decently, and have the moral capacity for exercise of the office for which they applied. One issue that divided opinions was whether recruitment should be local, regional, or national. Those who spoke in favor of local or at least regional recruitment deemed judicial knowledge of local customs and idioms important. The antagonists noted the disadvantages, including potential embarrassment by family considerations, personal ties, or simple social relationships, if a judge were a native of the area. No rule was established, but local selection was most often the norm during the nineteenth century.[17] Of course one point was completely ignored during this period—that of the right for women to enter the magistrature. Women were not permitted to serve until the law of April 11, 1946. These requirements[18] describe but part of a portrait of a modern judge.

During the nineteenth century three other criteria for appointment were also discussed, including personal fortune, intellectual capacity, and political opinions. The requirement of a personal fortune was a major theme in the nineteenth century. Many statesmen believed that a rich judge would be an attentive defender of private property, a guarantor of social conservatism, and a factor in cohesion.[19] Recruiting only rich judges, however, was obvious discrimination. Successive regimes combined three methods to achieve the goal: no remuneration or only a modest one for a beginning judge,[20] and then low salaries,[21] and advancement predicated on one's fortune.[22]

Napoleon wished to attract sons of the wealthy judicial families of the *Ancien Régime*; he also wanted to form young judges by placing them in contact with experienced jurists. To fulfill both objectives he created a novitiate by the decree of March 16, 1808. The requirement of considerable fortune became official, as a candidate was required to have a personal revenue of 3,000 francs per year and would be paid only one-fourth of the salary paid to a counsellor (a truly insignificant sum). These provisions were considered so aristocratic that they were eliminated on December 10, 1830. Then the function of assistant judge, which had been created by the law of *ventôse* 27, eighth year of the Republic (March 18, 1800), was altered from its initial purpose and became the first degree in the magistrature. A very low salary was established in 1910. During the nineteenth century a person could remain an assistant judge for seven or eight years. Obviously only wealthy young men could possibly enter a career without any income for so long. In the provinces more than one notable with a law diploma accepted this situation as an honor and remained in the same position for his lifetime.

Low salaries, which provided an inadequate living, implied the requirement of a personal fortune. What could appear as scandalous policy was presented quite cunningly, by emphasizing that the magistrate occupied an honorable position in society and sought only a moral satisfaction, not material ones, for his labors. In 1832 a deputy explained that this situation was quite normal even for ie judge who did not have a personal fortune. The profession necessitated absolute impartiality, and such a state of mind required that one live removed from the world, not spending much. Undoubtedly some candidates entered the magistrature for the title, while others at the beginning of the nineteenth century considered that the remuneration was just a compensation for all they had lost during the Revolution.[23]

Possession of a solid fortune was an argument for requesting—and often obtaining—an advancement. In 1823 there was the famous example of the Baron de Boussairolles, who did not hesitate to remind those in power that, besides 200,000 francs of revenue per year, he also owned the most beautiful house in Montpellier (the ancient palace where the provincial states of Languedoc once sat before the Revolution). Judges' personal fortunes diminished in importance during the nineteenth century, and by the end of the century the democratization of the magistrature implied that a person without any wealth could serve. Thus the requirement of a personal fortune was finally abandoned. Today, few judges are personally well-off; as salaries remain low, this is a problem.

The second debate, that of the intellectual capacity of a judge, had a positive conclusion. Before a text was even imagined, judges had to be nominated quickly. The government managed to obtain ample information on possible candidates with the help of the police (spies of the Ministry of the Interior and investigations by the Ministry of Justice).[24] As soon as the judicial machinery was in place, there would be time for elaborating legislation.[25] The first intellectual quality desired was maturity. The other requirement was judicial training. Law degrees had no better reputation at the beginning of the nineteenth century than they had in the *Ancien Régime*. The ideal was to find a select few, but the mode of achieving that aim caused a famous debate of the nineteenth century that was not easily resolved.[26] Of course, a minimum age was fixed. The law of April 20, 1810, provided that for a tribunal, the age was twenty-five for a judge or an assistant judge and twenty-seven for the president; in a court of appeal the age was twenty-seven for a counsellor and thirty for a president. Curiously, the ages required were lower in the Prosecution Department: in a tribunal, twenty-two years to be a substitute and twenty-five to be the head of the Prosecution; in the court of appeal, twenty-five for the substitute and thirty for the head of the Prosecution. In 1930 the ages were slightly reduced. The legislation established did not allow any exceptions, which was not surprising, as some already considered those recruited to be too young. But this was not the essential problem. Emphasis was placed on the practice of law. The first text, the law of *ventôse* 29, twelfth year of the Republic (March 20, 1804), allowed an attorney, who did not have a law *licence*, to enter the magistrature after having practiced as such for ten years. Even the law of April 20, 1810, required that to become a judge, one must have a law *licence* and have two years' experience as a lawyer. Napoleon was so convinced of this necessity that he had created, as mentioned earlier, a novitiate, which was later criticized and progressively replaced by competitive examinations.

Napoleon's first initiative[27] resulted in the decree of March 16, 1808. He decided to place auditor judges (*juges auditeurs*) in each court of appeal, so that they could complete a term of probation. The law of April 20, 1810, changed their titles to auditor counsellors (*conseillers auditeurs*). The candidates were required to have a revenue of 3,000 francs per year and two years' experience as lawyer. Auditor counsellors were appointed by the government from a list presented by the court to which they would be assigned. They could serve either in the Prosecution Department or on the bench. Eventually they could be sent to the lowest tribunals. Until they reached the required age, they had a consultative voice, but afterward, a deliberative voice. At the end of their terms they could be integrated into the magistrature. Surprisingly, the decree of April 20, 1810, created a new category of auditor judges, destined to be sent to tribunals having only three judges, and required that they have experience as lawyers. Many counsellor judges appear to have been nominated from the outset. On the contrary no auditor judge was appointed until 1814, and few were appointed from 1814 to 1820. After an ordinance of November 19, 1823, which enlarged their field of action, there were so many auditor judges that the tribunals became overstaffed. The youth and lack of experience of the auditor judges were noteworthy. After the Revolution of 1830 the institution in general was criticized because, in addition to other critiques, it had aristocratic origins. Auditor judges were referred to as a bastard magistrature, a school of idleness, inexperience, and compliance to power. The law of December 10,

came arbitrary and sometimes most unexpected. The simple mechanism of official propositions was completely circumvented by the private proceedings of those with political influence.

Reactions to these practices were rapid.[42] As early as 1839 an anonymous booklet was published proposing a table of advancement (*tableau d'avancement*), which was quite similar to the system that was to be adopted in 1906. At that time, however, the proposal gained little attention. In 1870 and 1892 other reform measures were submitted by deputies without success. Nevertheless the minister of justice finally proposed the first table of advancement in an administrative note of September 27, 1895. Unfortunately he was dismissed on November 1, 1895, and his successor suppressed the concept. The decree of August 18, 1906, definitively introduced the reform. The Ministry of Justice created a commission of the table of advancement. The commission was composed of the directors of the chancellery, the first president and the head of the Prosecution Department of the *Cour de Cassation*, and four members of the *Cour de Cassation*, who were nominated each year by the minister. This commission examined the propositions emanating from the first president and the head of the Prosecution of the courts of appeal. A judge could seize the commission directly by complaining that he had not been proposed. With this system the government did not retain absolute power, but still maintained control in three ways: the directors of the chancellery spoke for him, the four members of the *Cour de Cassation* designated by the minister were in his obedience, and the rules did not hinder the minister from modifying the list submitted by the commission of the table of advancement. Furthermore, although the government could not promote a judge whose name was not on the list, neither was the government obliged to promote a judge even if his name was on the list. In short, inclusion on the list did not assure a promotion, and this situation could repeat itself for years. The highest offices in the magistrature were not filled in this way. A decree of July 21, 1927, defined the judicial hierarchy, which facilitated promotion and modified the entire system. Thereafter, the first president of the *Cour de Cassation* was automatically the president of the commission of the table of advancement, and he determined its composition. Moreover, every judge on the list was assured of a promotion eventually. An effort was made to give less importance to the choice (*le choix*) and more to seniority. The executive lost much of its power, which it vainly sought to recuperate. Under the Vichy government the table of advancement was suppressed; it was reestablished by an ordinance of April 13, 1945. The constitution of October 27, 1946, changed nothing concerning the Prosecution Department, but it did innovate for the bench by creating the *Conseil Supérieur de la Magistrature*. This body determined promotions for the bench. The *Conseil* was composed of the president of the Republic, the minister of justice, six personalities elected for six years by the National Assembly, four judges elected by their colleagues for the same period, and two members designated by the president of the Republic. This arrangement was harmonious in that neither the magistrates, nor the representatives of the executive, nor those of the legislative power had a majority. Co-optation, so common in the *Ancien Régime*, was avoided, and the arbitrariness of the executive was significantly curtailed. This system was accepted with a degree of relief at a time when the nature of the magistrature had changed. During the nineteenth century most judges had been wealthy and did not require promotions. Democratization of the judiciary at the turn of the century made promotions financially necessary.

The principle of paying a salary to judges was affirmed when Bonaparte reorganized the judiciary.[43] The laws of *ventôse* 7, eighth year of the Republic (March 18, 1800), the decrees of July 16, 1804, June 20, 1806, and January 30, 1811, established low salaries. An administrative assembly, the *Conseils Généraux*, in the departments immediately criticized this policy. At one time Napoleon had thought of paying judges by the number of cases they considered. Those who worked hard would be paid substantially more than the others. This idea was abandoned, and the judges received meager remuneration throughout the nineteenth century. This situation created awkward practices, in that a judge often supplemented his income with a small extra job that did not conflict with his position. Three reforms (in 1846, 1862, and 1883) tended to improve judicial salaries. These reforms benefited judges in the first-degree jurisdictions and in the courts of appeal in the provinces such that between 1800 and 1883 their wages increased threefold. This policy reduced the differences between very low and high salaries, but the result was still unsatisfactory. In 1919 more adjustments were made, which were followed by others. Assimilation into the civil service progressed, such as allotments to judges for their residences and family expenses. In this sequence of events the constant concern was to ensure that judges were not paid less than were other civil servants. Undoubtedly this salary policy was an obstacle to recruitment of high-quality jurists. There were, however, advantages upon retirement.[44]

When the modern magistrature was organized, common practice was that a judge stayed in office for his lifetime. The legal justification was based on the principle of irremovability, but the practical result was not desirable. Jurisdictions were filled with too many elderly judges. One example, among others, was the case of Henrion de Pansey, who was appointed first president of the *Cour de Cassation* in 1828 at the age of eighty-six. The notion of retirement was not considered as a rule. The decree of October 2, 1807, provided that judges who became blind or deaf or who suffered from severe infirmities, which rendered them incapable of fulfilling their duties, could ask to retire and would be granted a pension. Such a disposition was, unfortunately, an exception. The law of June 16, 1824, established a reverse possibility, which explains the heavy procedure assuring solid guarantees to the affected judges. Two commissions composed of magistrates of the court of appeal collected information on "serious and permanent infirmities" impeding a judge from exercising his functions. The minister of justice would also make an inquiry. All three conclusions had to be similar to pronounce retirement for an ailing jurist. This procedure was seldom applied.[45] No wonder judges were astounded when the decree of March 1, 1852, set age limit: seventy for all judges except those in the *Cour de Cassation*, who retired at seventy-five. This measure was not popular because it was considered as an indirect means of dismissing judges from the preceding regimes—an assertion that was valid. The solution later became obvious as the right to retire became viewed as an advantage. The law of August 18, 1936, lowered the age limit by five years.

As magistrates could no longer rely on their salaries until the end of their lives, a pension was necessary for financial security. A complete reform for pensions was progressively legislated with the laws of June 9, 1853, April 14, 1924, and September 20, 1948.

Further, since the ordinance of August 17, 1824, there had been a recognition that judges' widows and orphans also had a right to a pension. This was consistent with the general system for civil servants.

If a pension was the rule for all, a distinction—the title of honorary judge—could be granted for personal merits. Napoleon I conceived of two possibilities: either the judge continued benefiting from the honors owing to his rank in ceremonies or he could also assist the general assemblies of his jurisdiction and have a deliberative voice. In 1852 this second category was eliminated.

The advantages at the end of a career, although very reasonable, were appreciated. However, if a judge were ambitious, he sought other advantages long before retiring. In the tradition of the philosophical theories and principles of the French Revolution, the separation of powers was maintained. Article 127 of the Penal Code of 1810 punished with forfeiture and civic degradation judges who interfered in the legislative field or in administrative matters. For those who thought they had goals other than simply being a judge, it implied that they assumed other functions. Either they served in several offices or they passed from one position to another.[46]

Hence, during the nineteenth century, judges exercised a direct influence on politics as members of local counsels in departments or as members of the legislative assemblies.[47] Simultaneous office-holding was legal. During the Monarchy of July the charter even provided that the king appointed the members of the *Chambre des Pairs* (House of Peers) from among the notables. On the list were magistrates belonging to the *Cour de Cassation* and to the courts of appeal for several years. Also, any judge could be elected as a deputy. This practice had positive consequences, in that the judges brought good advice based on their experience each time a law (particularly those relating to the judiciary) was debated in the assembly. Moreover, the judges gained in prestige and reinforced their moral authority. But there were also inconveniences. Judges who wanted to be appointed or elected would vie with one another, which did not correspond to their image of dignity. Once in the legislative assemblies, judges often neglected their judicial duties and often lost a portion of their independence by attempting to satisfy the king or the electors. Perhaps these negative aspects explain the decree of February 2, 1852, which forbade the accumulation of public offices. There was an exception for the first president and the head of the Prosecution Department in the *Cour de Cassation* and in the court of appeal of Paris.

Other judges abandoned the magistrature. Some assumed administrative functions, such as prefect of police or general director of the ministry of the police. Some sought political positions and became prefects in a department, minister (particularly minister of the justice), or even president of the Republic.

Magistrates who did not desire another career generally hoped that their merits would be recognized and rewarded with a decoration.[48] Bonaparte instituted the *Légion d'Honneur* in the tenth year of the Republic, and from *fructidor* 10, twelfth year of the Republic (August 28, 1804), this distinction was given to judges of the *Cour de Cassation*. A decree of October 18, 1811, even created a special decoration for services in the judiciary (*l'Ordre impérial de la Réunion*). During the Restoration the decorations of the *Ancien Régime* were re-established, but with the Monarchy of July, the *Légion d'Honneur* returned to favor and remains so today.

All of the advantages and prerogatives just described could entice a young man and lead him to enter the magistrature, but he had to be aware of the disadvantages as well. As a consequence of the principle of appointment by the executive, judges were ruled more severely than before.[49] The law of April 20, 1810, required that the magistrates live in the town where they held their positions. At first the law did not really appear as a problem, since judges who were recruited were generally local. The obligation of residence took a new dimension if one desired to advance, since that necessarily entailed moving from one jurisdiction to another.

The principle of executive control was far more annoying. The *sénatus-consulte* of *thermidor* 16, tenth year of the Republic (August 4, 1802), created the *Grand Juge* minister of justice, who was viewed as a sort of replica of the chancellor (minister of justice) of the *Ancien Régime*, since he had the right to control all the tribunals and their members. He then presided at the *tribunal de cassation*, which acted as a disciplinary jurisdiction. This tribunal could suspend a judge and order him to explain his attitudes. In 1883 this body was named *Conseil Supérieur de la Magistrature* and remained in force until 1946. There were many disciplinary proceedings based on the political attitudes of judges, particularly during the Monarchy of July[50] and at the end of the nineteenth century. The constitution of October 27, 1946, took the name *Conseil Supérieur de la Magistrature* to designate a totally new institution on which only the bench depended thereafter.

Members of the Prosecution Department were even more closely watched. The law of April 20, 1810, forbade them to leave their homes without obtaining an official permission, violation of which resulted in a sanction. More important, they had to obey the orders they received from the minister of justice because theoretically he had asked for the sovereign's advice. Therefore, they were forced to begin a prosecution that was required by the minister, but they remained free to conclude it according to their best judgment. In this context the adage of the *Ancien Régime*, "*La plume est serve, mais la parole est libre*" ("My pen is servile, but my word is free"), took on new importance. The minister could not, however, forbid a prosecution. The minister had several means of exercising his authority. He could demote, transfer, or remove any member of the Prosecution Department. Indeed, there were several famous examples of removal for political affairs during the nineteenth century, during the Monarchy of July, Second Empire, and Third Republic. Of course, the Prosecution Department was, and still is, a particular case. But since a judge could switch from the bench to the Prosecution and *vice versa*, all of the problems mentioned were not minor. The question arises inevitably of how were the judges face to the executive power.

THE JUDGES AND EXECUTIVE POWER

Bonaparte measured the dangers of appointment by the executive but balanced that feature with the principle of irremovability. The facts proved that this system gave no stability to judges and turned the judiciary into an instrument of dependency. Progressively another principle, that of the obligation of reserve, was formulated. Instead of just forbidding judges from adopting a position contrary to the government's policy, this principle also became a means of supervision.[51] Confronted by these two principles, the judges lost all illusions of independence.

The principle of irremovability was inherited from the *Ancien*

Régime and applied only to magistrates sitting at the bench. It assured their independence and dignity and appeared as a token of capacity, since the judges, certain to remain in office, did not hesitate to increase their knowledge. Curiously, Bonaparte did not proclaim this principle clearly in the constitution of 1799. He wrote two articles that, taken together, gave the same result. Article 41 declared that the *Premier Consul* appointed judges without the possibility of removing them. Article 68 provided that judges remain in office during their lifetimes, unless they were not maintained on the lists of eligibles. Later four constitutions (the charter of June 4, 1814, the charter of August 14, 1830, the constitution of November 4, 1848, and the constitution of October 27, 1946) expressly recognized the principle.[52] It was conceived differently by each regime.[53]

During the Restoration the king interpreted the principle from the perspective of the *Ancien Régime*. At that time the magistrate was viewed as a delegate to administer justice in the king's name. Therefore, he was irremovable as long as the king lived; at the king's death the mission of the judge also ended, unless the successor reconfirmed it. Therefore, in 1814, King Louis XVIII was absolutely not obliged to recognize judges named by the emperor Napoleon I. Logically, when Charles X succeeded his brother Louis XVIII in 1824, he was not obliged to maintain the judges appointed under the preceding reign, but he had no political reason not to confirm them.

Traditionally, the principle of irremovability had always been linked to the monarchy. This disturbed some politicians after the fall of the Monarchy of July, and as a consequence a decree of April 17, 1848, proclaimed the principle to be incompatible with a republican government. Thus began a lively exchange of views, but finally the constitution of November 4, 1848, recognized the principle.

In 1883 a new debate on the question opened in specific terms. It was to decide whether the principle was constitutional or not. Senator Jouin defended the theory of constitutionality. He claimed that the laws of the First Empire and the Restoration consecrated a personal link between the judge and the sovereign, whereas the constitution of 1848 proclaimed the principle as one to be respected by all true republicans and all people respectful of the law.

Thus the principle had been recognized as constitutional in the French system, and there was no reason to reconsider it. The minister of justice objected that the constitutions cited had been abrogated. Only the constitution of 1875 was valid, and that document remained silent on the point. He concluded by saying that the principle of irremovability was in the hands of the legislative power, which was free to act as it wished. This argument prevailed, and the Third Republic, like all the regimes of the nineteenth and twentieth centuries, disregarded the principle of irremovability.

Infringements on the principle of irremovability always had political motivations.[54] At each change of regime the executive power managed to obtain control of the magistrature by "purges." The means used varied, depending on the circumstances. Some were direct. One direct means was to give a specific interpretation of the principle. This enabled Louis XVIII to remove 294 magistrates between 1815 and 1818, all judges appointed during the First Empire. Another direct means was to suspend the principle; hence the purges. Less important were the purges in 1848 at the beginning of the Second Republic (only fourteen judges), and at the beginning of the Third Republic in 1871 (only fifteen). The most massive purge in the whole nineteenth century was an application of the law of August 30, 1883, when 614 judges, regarded as hostile to republican ideas, were eliminated in three months. Some modern authors liken this episode to the American "spoils system."[55] The same law was used to expel from the magistrature all the judges who had participated in the "*commissions mixtes*" to judge political affairs, which were established after the *coup d'état* of December 2, 1851. This body had pronounced about 15,000 condemnations in four weeks, which aroused sad memories thirty years later. Under the Vichy regime the law of July 17, 1940, provided that the magistrates, like the other civil servants, could be released from their functions because of their liberal opinions (ninety-one judges were removed). The law of August 11, 1941, decided that the dignitaries of secret societies would be removed, and affected forty-one judges. After the Liberation the ordinance of June 27, 1944, declared that all civil servants, inclusive of judges, who had favored the enemy's enterprises or who had disregarded constitutional institutions or fundamental public liberties would be subject to disciplinary sanctions.

Other methods were more indirect. After the Revolution of July, 1830, the leading political personages were jurists, who had no intention of altering the principle of irremovability. Nonetheless, in order to calm people's concerns, they passed a hypocritical measure. They obliged judges to pledge allegiance to the new regime and if they refused, they were considered as having resigned. There were refusals by 153 judges.[56] Later, when the prince-president (future Napoleon III) came into power, the decree of March 1, 1852, fixing the age of retirement, was used as a means of eliminating the old magistrates who were not favorable to his government. Consequently, 132 were removed. Another decree of March 8, 1852, required an oath in the same terms as that of 1830.

What is more exceptional is that twice regimes decided to get rid of some of their own magistrates. During the First Empire the *sénatus-consulte* of *thermidor* 16, tenth year of the Republic (July 30, 1802), suppressed the lists of notables. Instead of assuring irremovability, this was a means of suspending it. The *Grand Juge* minister of justice required a report, after which the *sénatus-consulte* of October 12, 1807, removed 162 judges. Although there was no change of regime, the reason was nonetheless political. Napoleon wished to affirm solidly his imperial government and to appeal to the old aristocracy. So he eliminated judges who had revolutionary backgrounds. Later, in the law of April 20, 1810, Napoleon decided to modify judicial terminology and restore the titles of the *Ancien Régime*, as, for instance, the word court instead of tribunal. On this occasion he proceeded to individual appointments for each court and profited from the movement to exclude more magistrates. The other regime that struck its judges was the government of Vichy. The law of June 2, 1941, forbade Jews to serve in judicial positions, thus eliminating eighty-nine judges.

All these examples lead to the conclusion that irremovability does not mean impunity. The sense of instability felt by the judges increased with the development of a notion known as "the obligation of reserve."[57] This notion is relatively modern. It would be vain to seek its origins in the *Ancien Régime*. Nonetheless many official speeches at that time referred to the dignity of the magistrate's condition, the love of his state, and the conscience of its solemnity. All of these concepts helped to create the doctrine during the nineteenth century.

The first basic documents were the law of *ventôse* 27, eighth year of the Republic (March 18, 1800), the *sénatus-consulte* of *thermidor* 16, tenth year of the Republic (August 3, 1802), and the law of April 20, 1810. They were the only legislative references to the obligation of reserve until 1883. They provided that a magistrate was committed to his obligations and could be disciplined if he failed to respect them. But what actions made one culpable? The *sénatus-consulte* mentioned "a serious fault," and the law of 1810 alluded to "reprehensible conduct" and "acts compromising the honor and dignity of the office." All these expressions were vague and enabled the executive power to interpret them arbitrarily.

The affairs judged between 1820 and 1880 were not numerous. Several famous proceedings took place under the Monarchy of July. Dupin, as head of the Prosecution Department of the *Cour de Cassation*, progressively elaborated a doctrine that was to serve as the reference during the nineteenth century. He argued that a magistrate had prerogatives as well as obligations. He claimed that a civil servant could not divide himself into two parts, that there could be no separation between a person's private life and official functions. He defined the disciplinary fault as any breach in the judge's conduct that caused him to neglect the character of dignity inherent in his position. The acts of primary focus were manifestations of hostility toward the government. Under the Monarchy of July the procedures sanctioned the conduct of "legitimists"[58] and republicans, whose public attitudes were well known. Detecting hostility to the government was not always that simple. Two administrative notes of May 15 and 18, 1850, demanded that each year the first president and the head of the Prosecution Department in the courts of appeal send to the minister of justice a report on all judges in their jurisdiction. They should note the fortunes, social status, and political conduct of each judge. A note of August 15, 1876, imposed supervision also on their writings. The vise was tightening. At the beginning of the Third Republic many disciplinary investigations were conducted, essentially against royalists, who were judged severely. The reference remained the doctrine fixed by Dupin, but a law was viewed as necessary. Such a law was passed on August 30, 1883. Article 14 of that law officially defined the "disciplinary fault" as all political deliberation of the judicial corporation and all manifestations of hostility toward the republican government, in its form or in its principle.

Throughout the different regimes judges felt more heavily the weight of the control exercised over them. That the process was irreversible was confirmed in the Fifth Republic in the ordinance of December 22, 1958, in which the term obligation of reserve is used for the first time (Article 10).

Confronted by an overwhelming executive power, the judges occupy a feeble position. The phrase Dupin pronounced at the Chamber of Deputies on November 26, 1830, merits consideration: "*Un juge qui craint pour sa place ne rend plus la justice*"[59] (A judge who fears for his employment no longer administers justice).

NOTES

1. This point was affirmed later in the law of April 20, 1810, creating the *cours d'assises*, which replaced the criminal jurisdictions.

2. Jean-Pierre Royer, *La Société judiciaire depuis le XVIIIe siècle* (Paris: P. U. F., 1979), pp. 249–50.

3. Marcel Rousselet, *Histoire de la magistrature française des origines à nos jours* (Paris: Plon, 1957), vol. I, p. 158; Royer, p. 247.

4. Jacques Godechot, *Les Institutions de la France sous la Révolution et l'Empire* (Paris: P. U. F., 1985), pp. 565, 73–74, 616; Rousselet, vol. I, pp. 158–59, 168, 206.

5. The *commune* or *arrondissement* was the lowest administrative unit. Each department was divided into four or five *communes*. Gérard Sautel, *Histoire des Institutions Publiques depuis la Révolution Française* (Paris: Dalloz, 1974), p. 298.

6. L. Duguit, H. Monnier, and R. Bonnard, *Constitutions et principales lois politiques de la France*, 7th ed. (Paris: L. G. D. J., 1952), pp. 120–28.

7. A. J. Tudesq, *Les Grands notables en France (1840–1849)*, (Paris: P. U. F., 1964), t. I.

8. Rousselet, vol. I, pp. 220–25; Royer, pp. 263–65.

9. Ibid., vol. I, pp. 161, 166, 168.

10. Ibid., vol. I, pp. 186–93.

11. The justice of the peace made his decisions alone, according to the

law of *ventôse* 29, ninth year of the Republic (March 20, 1801). He was considered as the exception in the general organization and was not involved in the debate. Rousselet, vol. I, p. 168. On the debate, see Rousselet, vol. I, pp. 160–61, 167, 204–6.

12. Ibid., vol. I, pp. 166–68.

13. Ibid., vol. I, pp. 187, 224; vol. II, pp. 130–31, 379.

14. Ibid., vol. I, pp. 194–97.

15. Ibid., vol. I, pp. 202–4; Royer, pp. 247–49.

16. A. Desjardins, *La Magistrature élue, La Revue des Deux Mondes* (Beauvais, 1882).

17. Christophe Charle, *Les Hauts fonctionnaires en France au XIXe siècle* (Paris: Gallimard-Julliard, 1980), pp. 123–24.

18. Rousselet, vol. I, pp. 217, 219–20, 229–31, 239, 253–57.

19. Royer, p. 281; Jean-Pierre Royer, Renée Martinage, and Pierre Lecocq, *Juges et notables au XIXe siècle* (Paris: P. U. F., 1982), pp. 139–47.

20. Rousselet, vol. I, pp. 181, 197–201, 227–28; Royer, p. 282.

21. Rousselet, vol. I, pp. 227; vol. II, p. 241; Royer, p. 281; Charle, pp. 125–26.

22. Rousselet, vol. I, pp. 227; Royer, p. 283.

23. Royer, p. 253.

24. Godechot, p. 618.

25. Rousselet, vol. I, pp. 234–36, 244.

26. Royer, pp. 275–76.

27. Rousselet, vol. I, pp. 181–82, 197–200; Royer, pp. 277–78; Jean-Pierre Machelon, *La République contre les libertés? (Paris: Presses de la Fondation Nationale des Sciences Politiques, 1976), pp. 90–92.*

28. Rousselet, vol. I, pp. 200–2.

29. Foucart, "De la nécessité d'exiger des candidats à la magistrature des conditions spéciales de capacité," La Revue de législation et de jurisprudence (October 1834–March 1835), pp. 346–57.

30. Rousselet, vol. I, pp. 206, 240, 248–51; Royer, pp. 278–80; Machelon, pp. 85–89.

31. Rousselet, vol. II, p. 134.

32. Ibid., vol. II, pp. 381–82.

33. Ibid., vol. II, pp. 163–64, 197.

34. Ibid., vol. I, p. 180; vol. II, pp. 99–100.

35. Ibid., vol. I, p. 179; Royer, pp. 254–55.

36. Rousselet, vol. I, p. 172; vol. II, pp. 130–33, 142, 145–46.

37. The functions of the Prosecution Department, which were dismantled in 1790, were reunited at the beginning of the *Consulat* (Godechot, p. 627; Sautel, p. 323).

38. Charle, pp. 131–32.

39. Royer, Martinage, and Lecocq, pp. 191–248.

40. Rousselet, vol. II, pp. 134–40, 143–44, 147; Royer, pp. 284–86.

41. Royer, Martinage, and Lecocq, pp. 33–49.

42. Rousselet, vol. I, p. 206; vol. II, pp. 144, 148–53.

43. Ibid., vol. II, pp. 133, 226, 236–42.

44. Rousselet, vol. I, pp. 177–78; vol. II, pp. 208–14.

45. Sautel, p. 530.

46. Rousselet, vol. II, pp. 366–67, 372–80; Royer, pp. 266, 269; Machelon, p. 99.

47. Royer, Martinage, and Lecocq, pp. 270–74; Charle, pp. 247–48.

48. Royer, Martinage, and Lecocq, pp. 162–67.

49. Rousselet, vol. I, pp. 168–69, 177, 210–13; vol. II, pp. 96–98, 200–3; Royer, pp. 288–89.

50. Marcel Rousselet, *La Magistrature sous la Monarchie de Juillet* (Paris: Sirey, 1937), pp. 363ff.

51. Royer, pp. 287–88, 304.

52. Rousselet, *Histoire*, vol. II, pp. 163–64; Royer, p. 250.

53. Rousselet, *Histoire*, vol. II, pp. 164–66; Royer, pp. 305, 314–15.

54. Rousselet, *Histoire*, vol. I, p. 208; t. II, pp. 166–71, 197; Royer, pp. 292, 305–11; Royer, Martinage, and Lecocq, pp. 317–75; Charle, pp. 236–39.

55. Machelon, pp. 281, 300.

56. Rousselet, *La Magistrature*, p. 63.

57. Rousselet, *Histoire*, vol. II, p. 368; Royer, pp. 287–300.

58. Legitimists were royalists faithful to the direct heir of Charles X and refusing to recognize his cousin Louis-Philippe as rightful king.

59. Rousselet, *Histoire*, vol. II, p. 174.

Chapter 6

Transatlantic Lessons

Experimentation with various systems for naming judges on both sides of the Atlantic have been reflections of national political cultures, or manifestations of distinct ways of "thinking about how politics and governing ought to be carried out."[1] The French and the American political cultures have conceived of political power differently for all major institutions of government—executive, legislative, administrative, and judicial. A complex of historical and ideological factors have shaped perceptions, symbols, and expectations differently. That these variations are mirrored in schemes to recruit judges should be expected.

French political history since the end of the *Ancien Régime* has been one of variety, lacking apparent continuity. Major upheavals and drastic alterations in the structure of government have been recurrent and typically are ideological or class-based.[2] The French Revolutionary motto of "equality and liberty" has retained adherents for almost 200 years. Yet there has also been a tendency to accept, even welcome, authoritarian regimes (as that of Bonaparte in 1799). Tensions within the political system have existed between privilege and equality or between individualism and administrative centralization.[3]

Consequently, since the end of the *Ancien Régime*, there have been five republican, three monarchial, and three "Bonapartist" constitutions for the French nation. Yet "this political instability was in strong contrast to the stability of its institutions, which," as de Lapradelle notes, "retained their fundamental features and improved them in more than one particular by a process of gradual evolution."[4] The essential stability of certain judicial institutions, particularly since the reign of Napoleon I, is notable. Reforms and refinements of the basic system designed by Bonaparte were tried or at least debated at various times, but the most salient elements of the institutions have not been dramatically altered. Elections for judges were, in 1791, a natural outgrowth of the ideals of the Revolution. Once rejected, however, return to that mechanism was never again able to gain sufficient support for its reinstatement. An appointed judiciary has been the prevailing norm for France since the beginning of the nineteenth century.

American political history was such that different issues have pervaded disputes regarding the judiciary. The first American state constitutions and the national constitution all embraced the concept of appointed jurists, appointed by the legislature or by the executive in tandem with the legislature. The history of America, unlike that of France, has been relatively stable and continuous in its evolution. The only major political upheaval was the Civil War, which proved not to be a sharp break with past practices, as the rebellious states were defeated.

In the development of the judiciary in the scheme of political power, there have been only three distinctive periods in American history. The first was the post-revolutionary era, which was both a reaction to and an appreciation of British traditions. The major deviation from the English heritage was a theoretical acceptance of the notion that the judiciary should be independent from the executive. That very independence, when it led to the invalidation of laws passed by legislatures, resulted in an extension of ideals of Jacksonian democracy to state benches. The period from Jackson's election to the Presidency until the Civil War is probably the only stage in American political life that was in some respects significantly influenced by ideology. The prevailing notion of the time was sovereignty of the people, and democracy, popular control of the instruments of political power. Democrats in the early part of the nineteenth century were not parallel to democrats in the twentieth century. The nineteenth-century democrat did not believe in the inherent goodness of man and, specifically, believed that man could be corrupted by power. "The central problem for eighteenth-century democrats, therefore, was how to protect the rights of the governed from subversion by their rulers."[5] Their answer was to make government weak, simple, and both immediately and directly responsible to the people.[6] The last objective was to be accomplished by frequent elections for all political officials, including judges.

The French and the Americans in the twentieth century have reached very different solutions for selecting jurists who will further societal goals. The current practices in each nation are, in some respects, simply variations on the themes that first emerged in the early nineteenth century. Yet the refinements of each system and the modifications that have occurred into the 1980s represent attempts to assign a place to the judiciary in the distribution of political power that is not inconsistent with each nation's political culture.

FRENCH JUDICIARY IN THE FIFTH REPUBLIC

The constitution of October 4, 1958, by proclaiming the irremovability of judges of the bench (Article 65)[7] and by requiring an oath of office,[8] marks the continuity of the present with the past. The constitution of the Fifth Republic settled two issues raised earlier. First, Title VIII specifies that judicial function is an authority and not a power.[9] Such a position might have been plausible during the nineteenth century, but today it does not seem to completely reflect reality. The jurisdictions, particularly the *Cour de Cassation*, have contributed to the evolution of French law by elaborating a substantial jurisprudence. For example, the importance of judicial interpretation can be observed in Article 1382 and subsequent provisions of the Civil Code, concerning liability for damages owing to malfeasance or nonfeasance.[10] This creative work could be viewed as affirming the judiciary as a power. Some jurists, however, do not agree.[11] The second important issue of the constitution is the announcement of a law organizing the judiciary (Article 65). Ordinance no. 58-1270 of December 22, 1958, as completed and transformed in 1967, 1970, 1977, 1979, and 1980, accomplished this task. This is one of the most remarkable elements of the judicial reform, for it consecrated the professional formation, the possibility that the judiciary may confront the executive power, and provision of a career.

The ordinance of December 22, 1958, instituted a *Centre na-*

tional d'Etudes judiciaires, which was designed to provide professional training for future magistrates.[12] Students entering the Center received the title of *auditeurs de justice*. The law of July 10, 1970, replaced the earlier institution with the *Ecole nationale de la Magistrature* (ENM). Admission to ENM is based on two competitive examinations. The first is solely for students who originally had to have a *licence en Droit* (delivered after four years of study). Since 1979, however, any diploma verifying completion of four years of study at a university is accepted. The second competitive examination is designed for civil servants who have served for five years. Interestingly, some people who do not fit either of these two categories can nonetheless enter ENM, with or without taking a test, if they have practiced law (for example, a minimum of three years for a lawyer). The training, which is partially academic and partially probationary, lasts for twenty-eight months. At the end there is an exit examination. Because all students pass this examination, some judges criticize the process as a useless exercise. Even so, the examination is maintained to be parallel with the final examinations of the *Grandes Ecoles* like *l'Ecole nationale d'Administration* (ENA) and to rank *auditeurs de justice* in order to facilitate their assignments.[13] Some will be assistant judges (this office was reintroduced by the law of October 29, 1980) but can serve in that capacity for no more than six years.[14]

The ENM is the mold through which all judges pass, whether they belong to the bench or to the Prosecution Department. This requirement is consistent with the unification of the judiciary, as it was officially consecrated in 1958.[15] Since that time the judiciary has been subject to the general rules (statute) of the civil service as modified by the specific principles studied here. One can serve on either the bench or the Prosecution, or switch between the two. This possibility can be regretted and has been the issue of many discussions.[16] The Prosecution offers a very different function and future from what may be anticipated on the bench. The Prosecution Department remains the "mouth" by which the government expresses its opinions,[17] and if the Prosecution receives an order to pursue a case, it must obey.[18] Furthermore, members of the Prosecution Department are not covered by the principle of irremovability and can thus be dismissed. The ordinance of December 22, 1958, created a disciplinary commission, which is invested with the function of protecting members of the department. The commission is composed of nineteen members, who are appointed for three years by the minister of justice, and is presided over by the head of the Prosecution Department of the *Cour de Cassation*. This commission is only advisory, and the minister of justice is free to follow its recommendation or not. In any case the members of the Prosecution Department have no ties to the *Conseil Supérieur de la Magistrature*, even when seeking a promotion. Thus the Prosecution Department is very different from the bench, but not sufficiently so to justify training other than at ENM.

Undoubtedly the ENM has become institutionalized. Its function is perhaps even more necessary now that a judge is often a solo decision-maker and, as such, does not benefit from the assistance of an older colleague. This is the case for the *juge d'instance* (judge of first instance) in first-degree jurisdictions and the *juge d'instruction*, who is the examining magistrate.[19] In August 1985 a reform was proposed for collegial decision-making at the level of *juge d'instruction*.

ENM is the normal means of entering the judiciary, but exceptions to the rule persist. As has always been the case, professors of law and persons belonging to judicial professions may enter the judiciary directly after a certain number of years of experience. The law of July 17, 1970, widened this possibility and provided for "lateral entry." As a result, between 1970 and 1977, 85 percent of the 432 magistrates recruited were lawyers meeting the requirement for length of practice. The more recent law of October 29, 1980, maintained provisions for lateral recruitment and even favored this route.[20] One can also be named as first president or head of the Prosecution Department of the *Cour de Cassation* by the *tour extérieur*, but such is a rare exception.[21]

Inevitably establishment of an academic institution such as ENM has consequences for the authority of the executive power. The Constitution of 1958 maintained the traditional principle of a judge's appointment by the head of the state. This prerogative is perhaps not as absolute as it once was, for the appointment of a judge at the beginning of his career is simply a confirmation of the results obtained at the ENM. Moreover, Article 66 of the constitution conferred a certain role to the *Conseil Supérieur de la Magistrature* regarding the appointment and discipline of judges.[22] The

Conseil makes propositions concerning the magistrates of the bench of the *Cour de Cassation* and the first president of the courts of appeal, but only gives advice on the names proposed by the minister of justice for other seats. Thereafter, the president of the Republic makes the appointment. There is a logical question about the ability of the *Conseil*, which might have views different from those of the executive, to intervene decisively in such a process, since the president of the Republic presides over and names all nine sitting members of the *Conseil*.[23] Three members are chosen from among the judges of the *Cour de Cassation*, three from the other courts and jurisdictions, one is *Conseiller d'Etat* (the *Conseil d'Etat* is the highest administrative court in France), and two are persons who do not belong to the judiciary. Some jurists interpret this process as the active participation of their corporation, since these appointments are relevant to the judges.[24] From this perspective, overriding the executive power is possible. Others, however, underscore the point that members of the *Conseil* have been designated by the president of the Republic and do not represent the judges. This procedure is not democratic. Such an interpretation has been adopted by the *Syndicat de la Magistrature*[25] and is a reaction against an omnipresent executive power.

The creation of the *Syndicat de la Magistrature* on June 12, 1968, was an extraordinary event.[26] This organization emerged as a consequence of the events of May 1968[27] and of a certain discontent among judges about how justice was administered. The ENM was considered as a factor in the development of such associations, since the *auditeurs de justice* were accustomed to collective discussion and action.[28] Since its creation the *Syndicat de la Magistrature* has condemned hierarchy in the judiciary as an excessive burden on a judge's position that obliges him to adopt a conformist attitude for the satisfaction of his superiors. On the other hand, the *Syndicat* considers the judiciary as but one element among others in the political world and attempts to transform the judiciary into a potential arena for political struggle.[29] This is relatively easy in cases concerning, for example, labor regulation and criminal offenses. The *Syndicat* presents a new way of conceiving the relationship between the judiciary and politics. The judiciary can be in conflict with the political powers. The *Syndicat de la Magistrature* has been perceived by some as subversive and as opposed to the established order. Such a view has given rise recently to a sense of alarm. Without prejudice, the issue should be examined by ascertaining the elements that determine the career of a judge, in order to detect potentially viable criticisms.

The normal judicial career consists of promotions within the judiciary. The rules were fixed in the ordinance of December 22, 1958, modified in 1967, and subsequently in the law of July 17, 1970, modified in 1980. The system is based on the establishment of a commission to elaborate the *tableau d'avancement.*[30] The commission is composed of twenty-one judges, issued of a second-degree election. All judges, in the extent of courts of appeal (except the first president and the head of the Prosecution Department), elect the members of the *Collège des Magistrats* for a three-year term. This body assembles in Paris and elects the judges who will be proposed for nomination in the *Commission d'avancement.*[31] When a promotion is discussed, the *Commission* takes heed of the individual judge's desires. He may be satisfied with a provincial career, or he might aspire to a post in Paris, with the goal of capping a career at the *Cour de Cassation.* Some authors note, without comment, that sometimes a career that once seemed blocked will suddenly open. Success is difficult and contingent on several elements, including not only one's knowledge and accomplishments, but also one's character, mode of living, and even style of dress.[32] The ordinance of July 12, 1962, fixed the age of retirement at seventy for members of the *Cour de Cassation* and sixty-seven for other jurisdictions. At the end of their careers, judges can obtain the *honorariat.* The law of October 29, 1980, extended the new rules and prerogatives of civil servants in general to the judiciary.[33]

The career outlined above is the normal scheme, but some judges, after several years in office, wish to profit from their experience by entering other arenas.[34] Judges are forbidden to simultaneously exercise another public office or any civil, commercial, or professional position, such as that of lawyer. If the magistrate has political ambitions, he might seek other offices, such as Parliament, the Parliament of the European Communities, or the *Conseil Economique et Social.* If a judge chooses any of these options, he must resign as a judge. However, there is no incompatibility between a judgeship and a local political position, such as that of *conseiller général* or *conseiller municipal*, so long as the judge does not exercise both offices in the same circumscription.

A simple analysis of the legislation since 1958 helps to explain the general profile of a judge today. In addition, sociological studies are essential for a comprehensive description.[35] The judiciary has been significantly feminized.[36] In 1959 women represented only 6 percent of the whole judiciary, in 1978, 18 percent, and according to projections, women should constitute more than 50 percent of the judiciary by 1990. This phenomenon presents at least two difficulties. On a general level, one consequence is a decline in the prestige of the judiciary, which could cause a crisis in attracting new judges. On a more personal level, there are complications when two judges decide to marry and each has a different geographical assignment. There still exists an anti-woman bias and, whether consciously or not, the juries at the ENM hesitate to interrogate women.

Also, the judiciary is aging. In 1948, 43 percent of the judges were between twenty-five and forty years of age and 20 percent between fifty-seven and seventy. In 1972 the proportions were reversed, with only 13 percent under forty and 37 percent over fifty-seven. The reason was a disaffection for the office of magistrate during that twenty-year interval. The pyramid of ages marked a need for judges born between 1929 and 1943. To facilitate the recruitment of such candidates, the government lowered the age of retirement and developed the system for lateral recruitment.

Social origins of judges are also changing. Among the 1,000 *auditeurs de justice* at the ENM between 1975 and 1979, there appears to be a drop in students from judicial families (they represented only about 5 to 8 percent), a consistency in number of students from civil servant families, and an increase in students from working-class families (6.6 percent).

In 200 years the judiciary has changed dramatically. Not all judges are satisfied with the present system. Very recently the president of the *Cour d'Assises* of Paris (the criminal jurisdiction in the department) resigned, quite solemnly. He protested against the criminal policy that created excessive impediments to proper administration of justice. He also denounced the dependence of the judiciary on the executive power and concluded by declaring that today only the American system respected the independence of judges, and therefore best represented the democratic principles.[37]

AMERICAN JUDICIARY IN THE 1980s

There are essentially two methods for selecting judges in the United States: appointment and election. However, the most common variations on these two basic themes result in a taxonomy of five different types of judicial selection mechanisms. Appointment may be by the governor of a state (or by the President for federal constitutional judgeships), by legislative election, or by merit selection/merit retention. Elections may be either partisan or nonpartisan. The modifications to each of these systems have been extensive. For example, Ohio holds partisan primary elections, followed by nonpartisan general elections.[38] Many states use more than one method of selection, varying by level of court. Also, states with elective systems may use different methods for filling vacancies that occur midterm owing to retirements, resignations, or deaths. The consequence of these multiple means of naming judges in each of the fifty states and for the national courts is a patchwork quilt. However, accepting the broad categories of five methods, the *Book of the States, 1984–1985* classifies fourteen states as ones using partisan elections, eighteen as using nonpartisan election, nine using gubernatorial appointment, three using legislative elections, and seventeen using merit selection/merit retention.[39] The total of sixty-one exceeds the actual number of states because more than one method may be used for different levels of courts.

Appointive systems were initially adopted by the states after the Revolutionary War. They are the systems used for naming federal judges since the ratification of the U.S. Constitution in 1791. Essentially, appointive systems entail nomination of a candidate for a judgeship by the executive (governor or President), which must be ratified by one or both houses of a legislature. Legislative election involves a simple election in a legislature to fill a vacant judicial position. Merit selection/merit retention (the so-called Missouri Plan) attempts to combine some electoral accountability with the basic notion of appointment, and this plan will be discussed later in some detail. The theory behind the appointive method is that the person or persons making the appointment will be held accountable for their choices. Theoretically, a governor who has a record of naming incompetent, corrupt, or overtly partisan judges to the bench would be called to account by the public when facing a re-election bid.

Little research has been done on the actual operation of appointive systems in the states. The primary criticism of the system is that appointments are used as patronage. Clearly, governors and Presidents name only members of their own party and often of their own political ideology to the bench. This has been the obvious tactic used by California governors since the tenure in that state of Ronald Reagan.[40] The more serious allegation against the appointive system is that "political hacks" who lack legal expertise and judicial temperment will tend to be named as a *quid pro quo* for prior political service.[41] Similarly, some contend that judges named by a governor or a President forfeit a degree of judicial independence because of their ties to the appointer.[42] Finally, although most appointed judges are named for a specific period of time, judges who desire an additional term will typically be granted that term and will in effect have life tenure in office.[43]

We know much more about the Presidential nomination of federal judges than we do about the appointing process at the state level. Typically, at least in this century, the President has not acted alone to make his nominations to the federal bench. The Justice Department, specifically the deputy attorney general, receives and screens applications and nominations for federal judgeships. Until the Carter and Reagan administrations the Justice Department usually worked with the American Bar Association to obtain rankings of possible judicial candidates, but Carter replaced the ABA's ratings with his own merit commissions,[44] and Reagan has chosen not to consult the ABA until after a nominee has been selected.[45] Once the President has settled on a nominee, the name of the candidate is sent to the Senate for confirmation. The Senate Judiciary Committee holds hearings on each nomination, including an appearance by the nominee before the Committee for questioning. A favorable vote by the Committee tends to be the norm, unless the senator from the state of the judicial position has a serious objection to the appointment (senatorial courtesy). Notable exceptions to this rule occurred with Nixon nominations of Haynesworth and Carswell to the U.S. Supreme Court—the Senate rejected both nominations. Different Presidents also have different agendas for their nominees. For example, President Carter emphasized the need for a representative bench through his nominations. Consequently, when he filled fifty-six vacancies on the U.S. Court of Appeals, he named eleven women, nine blacks, two Hispanics, and one Asian-American. President Reagan has indicated a different bias, one that is ideological. He favored nominees who were conservative in their political outlooks; being anti-abortion was said to be his litmus test for judicial appointments.[46]

The merit selection/merit retention plan has become the most popular means for designating judges in the American states and has been endorsed by the American Bar Association and the American Judicature Society. The system is typically called the Missouri Plan, since that state was the first to adopt the process in 1940. Essentially, it calls for the creation of a commission with representatives from the bar and from the public, with one sitting judge. The attorneys are to be named by the bar association, and the laypersons are to be chosen by the governor. This group is charged with screening potential judicial candidates and recommending three to the governor. The governor appoints one person from the list to a one-year term of office. At the conclusion of that year (or at the next general election) the appointee must be confirmed by the electorate. There is not an opposition candidate, but rather the judge "runs on his record." Voters are asked to vote yes or no to retain Judge X. If the judge receives an affirmative vote, he will serve for a lengthy term (usually six to twelve years), at the conclusion of which he must once again go before the voters for confirmation. According to Carbon, therefore, the goals of the system are met.

> The reformers who conceived the idea vest it with two principal purposes: lengthy tenure for judges and public accountability. Because judges would be chosen initially on the basis of professional merit, reformers anticipated very few removals by the electorate and only in egregious cases.[47]

Two critical assumptions underlie the merit selection/merit retention plan. The first is that the commission will guarantee the professional competence of judges; the second is that retention elections can ensure public accountability.[48] The former assumption can be challenged on several grounds. Among the allegations are that the commissions give disproportionate influence to the established bar and that commissions tend to be composed of white men who are not inclined to nominate women or minorities. Even the commissioners themselves do not pretend that partisan politics have been removed from the screening process.[49] The ability of retention elections to provide public accountability is questionable, in that only one percent of all judges who have faced retention elections have been removed by the electorate.[50] Thus, those who are appointed by the governor are virtually assured (short of committing a serious public crime) lifetime tenure.

Judicial elections are the means of achieving complete public accountability. Reformers in this century have suggested that one means of improving the quality of the judiciary would be to remove political parties from the process. Therefore, the nonpartisan election was introduced in which candidates' names appear on the ballot without a political party label. As noted previously, many states have chosen to retain partisan races and continue to have judges run as Democrats or as Republicans. Despite the use of elections as the formal means of filling judicial vacancies, many judges under this system are initially appointed by the governor for midterm vacancies. Indeed, between 1948 and 1974 half of all supreme court justices in northeastern states with an elective system were filled by gubernatorial appointments.[51] This is not atypical.

Elections for judges, as for other officials, have certain assumptions at their base. Theoretically, the direct effects of elections are expected to be that the voters influence public policy through their ballots. Indirectly, elections invest the institutions of government with legitimacy and power. Even though elections for most offices are limited in achieving these goals, they can accomplish other aims. One of these is the retrospective pronouncement of the public on the performance of officeholders. Presumably officials who do not perform at a level expected by the public will be removed.[52]

For these assumptions to be viable there are necessarily expectations that voters are rational and informed people who cast their ballots knowledgeably. Judicial elections receive their harshest indictments on this count. Studies have demonstrated that voters tend to know very little about judicial races,[53] partially because campaigns are lackluster and devoid of issues, owing to limitations imposed by canons of judicial ethics. Voters tend to rely on cues, as opposed to concrete information, when casting their ballots for judges. These cues are often candidate attributes that are discernible from the ballot—party, ethnicity, sex, incumbency, name familiarity, or even use of nicknames.[54] Ballot labels indicating a candidate's occupation were recently found to be predictive of the proportion of votes to be won at the polls.[55] Voter information that is available from sources other than the ballot has also been found to determine election outcomes. Specifically, bar poll ratings and newspaper endorsements affect who wins and who loses judicial races.[56] The issues raised by these findings relate to the extent to which voters are able to make rational and informed choices among judicial candidates. A second question about the viability of judicial elections as a means of achieving accountability is the vast success of incumbent judges at the polls. Challenged incumbents tend to win judicial elections,[57] but more importantly, most sitting judges do not face any opposition in their re-election bids.[58] A final allegation against judicial elections is the necessity for campaign funds to seek the office. Reliance of judicial officers on the contributions of attorneys or of public affairs committees of various organizations potentially carries the taint of partiality in cases involving contributing attorneys or contributing organizations.

Virtues and vices are apparent in all of the systems used to designate judges for federal courts and for state benches. None appears to achieve all of its stated goals completely, and all appear to have the potential to compromise judicial impartiality. What is more interesting is that there is no evidence to support the proposition that any one of these systems produces a "better" judge than do others. Academic backgrounds and prior judicial experience tend to be approximately the same for judges selected under each system.[59] Appellate court judges selected under the various systems do not appear to make decisions that differ in any systematic fashion.[60]

Judges in the American states tend to follow some consistent patterns, regardless of the formal system by which they were selected. Because of fifty years of Democratic dominance, the majority of all trial judges identify with that party. The average judge was forty-six at the time he assumed his office. The trial bench is basically white and male, with 96 percent of all judges meeting these two criteria.[61] The number of women and minority judges is, however, increasing, and there is a tendency toward younger judges. Whether these trends will continue in the future is another question. Loss of income, loss of personal freedom, and limitations on business activities tend to deter many practicing attorneys from considering judicial offices.[62] These barriers, more than the method of selection, may be responsible for the absence of quality on the bench.

COMPARATIVE ANALYSIS

The contemporary legal systems of France and the United States, although very different in both content and administration, spring from common roots. In the twelfth and thirteenth centuries French and English law were quite similar, as the kings attempted to fashion systems of royal law. Although many contrasts between Anglo-American and French law have developed, common and civil law share common roots.[63] Today the distinctions between Anglo-American common and French civil law are not so dramatic in practical terms as some would suggest.[64]

Max Weber contended that domination is the primary factor in political power, and that law is one means used to achieve domination through coercion. The differences among diverse legal cultures, he contended, "were largely dependent upon political factors" (i.e., political power).[65] Harold Berman, writing more recently, would concur with Weber but would add other factors to the equation explaining different legal cultures. Law does reflect socioeconomic facts, but "it is also idea, or concept, and, in addition, it is a measure of value."[66] Therefore, legal systems necessarily reflect economic, social, moral, ideological, and intellectual values.[67]

The evolution of a system of law and legal culture is dependent not only on the lawgiver, but also on the law interpreter or judge. As a consequence, who is designated to interpret and administer the law is extremely relevant in a culture's legal development and is a reflection of political power relationships. In other words, the three stages of political recruitment proposed by Seligman—certification, selection, and role assignment—are of considerable relevance for the designation of jurists in Western legal cultures.[68] The evolution of the French and American systems for designating judges since the eighteenth century demonstrates a recognition on the part of constitutional and legal draftsmen of the critical importance of who serve as judges for ideology, practicality, and political power. Attempts to balance the requirements of ideology, politics, and legal competence characterize the development in each country.

Seligman and his associates' three-stage process of recruitment offers an appropriate matrix for comparison of how judicial elites have been named in France and in the United States. The certification stage, as you may recall, involves sorting the most likely candidates from among the larger pool of those who are formally and effectively eligible. For any political office, including judgeships, "the selection process does not operate randomly; candidates who are prominent emerge from a pool of eligible individuals."[69] Eligibility has sometimes been defined in legal terms but almost always includes a number of ascriptive characteristics that are unwritten. In the United States the legal qualifications for jurists have sometimes included legal training, but not always. The informal requirements have, however, always entailed expectations that led to a middle or elite class bias. Schmidhauser[70] and Hall[71] have demonstrated this historical tendency among federal judges; Ryan and his associates confirmed a similar trend among current trial court judges. Likewise, until the mid-1970s, certification for judicial office was largely reserved to middle-aged white males.[72]

The formal requirement of legal training was not incorporated into statutory law in the United States until the firm establishment of bar associations. Lay judges formed a traditional component of the bench in America and were, at the beginning of the nineteenth century, sometimes preferred, as anti-lawyer sentiments were prominent. Definitions of "legal training" or "legal knowledge" were variable by state and by county until this century, when law schools and bar entrance requirements became prevalent in all states.

In France, certification was, under the *Ancien Régime*, partly a question of economic capacity, as judges purchased their offices. Under subsequent revolutionary regimes even legal training was rejected as a formal criterion for the bench, since, in the tradition of Rousseau, every man could administer justice. This idea baffled law faculties, but this is comprehensible, since many were of low standards. In the United States, on the other hand, the absence of established university training in law made requirements of legal knowledge dependent on length of legal experience, not on diplomas or licenses. As the French experimented with their judicial department throughout the nineteenth century, a number of ascriptive criteria were formalized but were not always the only criteria. Wealth, legitimacy of birth, nobility, and fortune intervened now and then. Clergy were barred from the bench at the time of the Revolution. Merit and knowledge were the desired qualifications. At times the desired social or political status was made explicit, but in other eras it was only implicit and was assured through somewhat circuitous routes.

The common factor for certification in France and in the United States, when jurists were politically appointed, was the "proper political persuasion." In America, political party affiliation or activity was a critical factor for naming judges. In France, because of the fluidity of parties, ideology and political inclinations of potential judges were assessed differently. Nevertheless, the appointing authorities consistently endeavored to name judges who would view the political world similarly. The French judiciary under the Fifth Republic, at least officially, does not consider political attitudes in recruitment of judges. Political party and perspectives on political power remain primary criteria in the United States, particularly for federal judgeships.

Selection, the second phase of recruitment, involves interaction among candidates, sponsors (including political parties), and the appointing body. Political party affiliation and activity have perennially been essential to attain judgeships in the United States. That trend is traceable in the federal judiciary since 1800, when the Federalists attempted to pack the judicial branch, to President Reagan's nominations of Rehnquist and Scalia to the highest federal court. The institution of elections to choose judges in the states initially heightened the role of political parties, which assumed the role of instigating or co-opting and sponsoring judicial candidates. Party primaries and nonpartisan elections have somewhat muted the control of political party organizations over the choice of judges. Nevertheless, partisan activity remains a crucial variable for gubernatorial appointments, even in states using the merit selection plan and those using elections. In the latter case, governors fill new judgeships and midterm vacancies and typically regard partisanship as an important criterion.

Sponsors and appointers in France have interacted with candidates in various ways over the past two centuries. Under the *Ancien Régime*, candidates for the magistrature courted the favor of judges on the bench to which he aspired and was, through a series of investigations and examinations, co-opted by his eventual peers. The first elected judges, except in the provinces, were people of prior political or judicial experience and were, therefore, reflective of the presiding regime. The influence of the appointing body on the judges was most obvious between the Revolution and the ascent of Bonaparte, in that if the mechanism in place for naming judges did not yield the desired results, the system (and the judges) was promptly changed. Because Bonaparte created confidence in the institutions of government, objections to executive appointment of judges subsided, and the basis of the present system of appointment was established. Potential candidates were co-opted in this system in consideration of their family backgrounds, which tended to be judicial or civil servant families. The formation of a novitiate was a means of socializing new jurists into the norms of their elder peers. Fathers sometimes resigned their positions in favor of their sons. Not until the judiciary was integrated into the civil service did sponsorship and co-optation cease to characterize the selection of French judges. Even now, as noted earlier, one's life style and choice of fashion can influence judicial promotions, which leads to conformity among those with ambitions for selection at higher levels.

Role assignment refers to the final stage of the recruitment process in which the successful candidate assumes his office. The oath of office constitutes official assumption of judicial duties in both the United States and France. Yet what that office means or what the judicial role entails has varied on both sides of the Atlantic. Despite the French principle of irremovability, judges were often insecure in their positions. Under the *Ancien Régime* there was the potential for having the office repurchased by the king. The various revolutionary governments created, abolished, and altered judgeships such that security in office was doubtful. Low or irregularly paid salaries necessitated that judges, in the nineteenth century, have personal fortunes, which might have created stability for those on the bench. Yet the political persuasion of a judge could result in his dismissal, as purges occurred throughout the nineteenth century and even in 1940 and 1941. Only in the Fifth Republic, with definitive rules organizing entrance to the judiciary based on competitive examinations and promotions predicated on the *tableau d'avancement*, have French jurists, since the *Ancien Régime*, had security in their offices. Some jurists feel, though, that their security has coincided with loss of independence through reliance on the executive power.

The judicial role in the United States has grown to connote something quite different. Judicial independence is a term often associated with the American judiciary. That description was not totally valid in the nineteenth century, as impeachment trials occurred and courts were abolished because of decisions that were not palatable to the legislatures. Some contend that popular elections also curtail judicial independence, as voters would oust a judge for an unpopular decision. The extent to which the electorate behaves in that manner or to which judges consider future elections in rendering decisions is obviously not capable of verification or refutation empirically. However, indications are that, barring major scandals, voters are not well informed about judges or judicial decisions. Rather, the greatest insecurity in office, both in the United States and in France, probably stems from the absence of rewards for judicial service. Since before 1800, lawyers in the United States have contended that judicial salaries made the offices unattractive. The loss of prestige has been lamented on both sides of the Atlantic.

Both French and American judges historically would dispute the characterization offered by Murphy and Tanenhaus: "Judges usually derive considerable political power from their participation in the processes of determining goals and allocating values in themselves. Because they carry power, they bestow prestige, as well as a comfortable living, on incumbents."[73] Despite the insecurities in office, judicial officers are important actors in the political arena.

TRANSATLANTIC LESSONS

In developed societies, multiple societal problems and issues are resolved through litigation. "Nowhere can judges keep out of the controversies of the times," explains Henry Ehrmann, in his consideration of the French judiciary. "They cannot help playing a political role."[74] French jurists are not inclined by role or by systematic limitations to be as politically active as American judges. Despite periods of judicial passivity in the United States, there has been a general inclination to enter the political thicket and confront problems that others have avoided. This is so much the case that Donald Horowitz contends that "no courts anywhere have greater responsibility for making public policy than the courts of the United States."[75] The power of American courts to exercise judicial review over actions of the other branches of government is usually seen as the source of this policy-making orientation. In that the French have reserved that function to the Council of State (*Conseil d'Etat*), French judges would not be expected to be equally active in the political life of their nation. Notably, however, the authority that was given to the judges in the United States and in France was determined politically and was consistent with societal views of the appropriate role of the judiciary. Ehrmann would suggest that French courts are unable to avoid making policy through the elaboration of a jurisprudence in areas not covered by codes and in the gaps in the laws. Horowitz would contend that the judicial role of the American judge is not a function of ascribed legal roles, but a result of the American "proclivity to think of social problems in legal terms and to judicialize everything from wage claims to community conflicts and the allocation of airline routes."[76] The conclusions that we are suggesting are two: both French and American judges are implicitly, if not directly, part of political life and political power by virtue of the issues that are settled in courts, and the political culture of each country has affected legal prescriptions regarding judges and the practical effects of judicial decisions.

The political cultures of the United States and of France have each influenced judicial institutions. The variety of types of judicial selection systems used in the American states is probably due to the variations of cultures from one region to another within the United States. The federal principle was adopted in the United States as a means of permitting diversity among the states. The differences from one region to another are, at times, so marked as to suggest that there are subcultures within the United States. Daniel Elazar has proposed that there are three distinct subcultures in the

United States—individualistic, moralistic, and traditionalistic—that are "strongly tied to specific sections of the country, reflecting the streams and currents of migration."[77] For example, the South is predominantly a traditionalistic culture, one with pre-commercial attitudes and an attachment to the *status quo*. The West, on the other hand, is dominated by a moralistic culture. The term moralistic is used to connote a perception of politics as a public activity designed to promote the public good and the advancement of public interest. There are difficulties, obviously, with any attempt to make such general classifications, but there is some evidence that methods for recruiting judges do tend to follow regional lines. The differences are so substantial from region to region that Dubois, in his study of elections of supreme court justices, excluded all Southern states from his analysis because he anticipated that these states would not be "typical."[78] Indeed, most Southern states have retained partisan elections for judgeships, whereas most Western states have, consistent with expectations of a moralistic culture, adopted merit retention and merit selection. The variations in political culture from one state or one region to another probably accounts for differences in judicial selection mechanisms in the United States.

France, of course, is a unitary state, with governmental functions such as recruiting judges handled centrally. Not only is this approach reasonable for a nation whose geographical area is approximately that of the state of Texas, but likewise is consistent with the entire political history of France. Granted that there are variations in perceptions about the business of politics from region to region and from the provinces to Paris. However, because of the centralized nature of the government, these differences are not directly manifested in matters of the judiciary.

Despite the various experiments in selecting judges in either culture, there have been persistent questions about the ability of any to attract and retain the desired caliber of judges. The assumption behind any formal selection mechanism is that people with particular characteristics will be named and others who lack those prerequisites will not.[79] Yet both the French and the Americans have frequently been disappointed in the people on the bench, who reach those positions through the prescribed system. In the United States there is little evidence to support the proposition that any of the various selection systems actually produces different mixes of judges.[80] The French found that elections, when there were no prescribed qualifications, produced judges who were lacking in professional competence (i.e., ones who were not even trained in the law). More recently, under the Fifth Republic, there has arisen a concern for the prestige of the judiciary as a consequence of an increased number of women. Both the United States and France have also confronted periodic concerns about the political disposition of judges. During the nineteenth century in the United States, many of the early reforms, specifically use of elections, were a reaction by state legislatures to the practice of judicial review as exercised by their supreme court justices. The French, during that era, altered retirement practices or applied the obligation of reserve in order to purge the bench of jurists of unacceptable political loyalties. The twin issues of professional competence and political outlook continue to affect, more or less, recruitment practices in both nations. The implementation of lateral entry was one means of securing desirable judges in France, as was the importance of the judgment of superior judges for a novice's advancement. At the federal level in the United States, every President, at least since Kennedy, has attempted to fill the bench with people who are of his political party. Presidents Nixon and Reagan refined the requirements even further, appointing only Republican judges who are "strict constructionists" or who adhere to notions of interpretation "according to the intent of the framers." That either system as currently practiced actually succeeds in obtaining competent judges who are likewise of the desired political persuasion is not clear.

Every system for designating judges is replete with imperfections. Further, there have been difficulties inherent in each system tried. Whereas many an American judge or attorney views the continental system as ideal because that process provides for training judges and for basing promotions on merit, the French bench has not been free of problems. A prominent example of the frustration that French judges perceive was the belief that judges needed a union to protect their interests from executive interference and from coercion by superior judges. The *Syndicat de la Magistrature* was founded in 1968, during the Events of May. Since that time the *Syndicat* has defended judicial independence and attempted to make public allegedly inappropriate administration of justice.[81]

Professional competence and ethics have become another concern in the United States. The practical irremovability of American judges under any system is the crux of the problem. Impeachment at the federal level has been a hollow threat, as only eleven federal judges have been impeached and only five were actually removed from office through that procedure.[82] Likewise, in the states most judges, whether they reach their positions through election, appointment, or merit selection, have virtually life tenure, barring some egregious public crime. This fact has led to a shift in emphasis from recruitment to removal.[83] That many sitting judges are not competent to perform their duties by reason of infirmity or ignorance and that at least a proportion of America's jurists have succumbed to corrupt influences are not in question.[84] Much of the confusion may be traced to an unsettled controversy over the precise place that the judiciary is to play in the balance of political power. Montesquieu's proposition that an independent judiciary was essential to the preservation of liberty was not fully comprehended at the conclusion of the eighteenth century and may not be understood at the close of the twentieth century. As long as judges are expected to be apolitical and above politics, but are confronted with cases involving basic societal values and allocation of political power, there may remain conflicts about the role of the judiciary.

Consideration of the proper place of the judiciary in the governmental structure inevitably raises the issue of qualifications, recruitment, and tenure of judicial officers. France and the United States have chosen different methods to resolve this conflict and to reduce the tensions. That either system might be transplanted to the other side of the Atlantic is neither likely nor desirable. Judicial systems, like law, grow out of that complex of political, economic, moral, historical, and ideological blend in each nation that is called political culture. A nation's political culture "filters perceptions, determines attitudes, and influences modalities" such that it is "a major component of the political game."[85] Those features of French political life that have evolved over almost 200 years, since the end of the *Ancien Régime*, culminate in an essential rejection of the overt or even muted politics that pervade all categories of American judicial behavior. However, to erase the American expectation that all attorneys are potentially qualified to be judges and to ignore the political role of the judiciary in American life would be to nullify 200 years of United States history. Transposing either process from one nation to the other would violate the "patterned set of ways of thinking about how politics and governing ought to be carried out."[86] Despite the merits or difficulties of any conception of the judiciary and the concomitant concept of how to name judges for that function, the likelihood that any single standard would flourish equally on both sides of the Atlantic denies the place of law and legal culture in a nation's consciousness.

NOTES

1. James Q. Wilson, *American Government: Institutions and Policies* (Lexington, Mass.: D. C. Heath & Co., 1986), p. 77.

2. Roy C. Macridis, "France," in *Modern Political Systems: Europe*, ed. Roy C. Macridis (Englewood Cliffs, N. J.: Prentice-Hall, 1983), p. 87.

3. Henry W. Ehrmann, *Politics in France* (Boston: Little, Brown & Co., 1982), p. 13.

4. A. de Lapradelle, "Law," in *Modern France*, ed. Arthur Tilley (New York: Russell & Russell, 1922), p. 351.

5. Richard E. Ellis, *The Jeffersonian Crisis: Courts and Politics in the Young Republic* (New York: Oxford University Press, 1971), p. 251.

6. Ibid.

7. Jean Vincent, Gabriel Montagnier, and André Varinard, *La Justice et ses institutions* (Paris: Dalloz, 1982), pp. 476, 501.

8. Ibid., p. 496.

9. Jean Foyer, "*Un Pouvoir refusé*," 16 *Pouvoirs*, (1981), pp. 17–18.

10. Ibid., pp. 26–27.

11. Michel Troper, "*Fonction juridictionnelle ou pouvoir judiciaire?*" 16 *Pouvoirs* (1981), pp. 5–15.

12. Vincent, Montagnier, and Varinard, pp. 484–88; Pierre Martaguet, "*Comment devient-on magistrat?*" 16 *Pouvoirs* (1981), pp. 108–12.

13. Martaguet, pp. 116–17.

14. Vincent, Montagnier, and Varinard, pp. 498–503.

15. Ibid., p. 477.

16. François Sarda, "*Le Pouvoir et les instances judiciaires*," 16 *Pouvoirs* (1981), pp. 75–76.

17. This principle is still turned round by the adage previously mentioned, "*La plume est serve mais la parole est libre*." Thus the *avocat général* (second in command to the head of the Prosecution Department), near the *Cour d'Assises* of Paris, addressed the court in severe terms at

the end of February 1986 and openly condemned the criminal policy of the minister of justice. "Judiciary chronicle of Pierre Bois," *Le Figaro* (March 1–2, 1986), p. 10.

18. Vincent, Montagnier, and Varinard, pp. 539–41, 555.

19. Michèle Giannotti, "*L'Agenda du magistrat, le siège*," 16 *Pouvoirs* (1981), pp. 120–21.

20. Vincent, Montagnier, and Varinard, p. 491; Jean-Luc Bodiguel, "*Qui sont les magistrats français? Esquisse d'une sociologie*," 16 *Pouvoirs* (1981), p. 33; Martaguet, pp. 112–13.

21. Etienne Bloch, "*Faire carrière sous la Ve*," 16 *Pouvoirs* (1981), pp. 101–2.

22. Vincent, Montagnier, and Varinard, pp. 476, 494–96.

23. The president of the Republic does not preside at the *Conseil Supérieur de la Magistrature* when it is convened as a disciplinary council. It is then presided over by the first president of the *Cour de Cassation*. Vincent, Montagnier, and Varinard, p. 522.

24. Foyer, p. 26.

25. Pierre Lyon-Caen, "*Le Syndicat de la Magistrature*," 16 *Pouvoirs* (1981), p. 59.

26. Vincent, Montagnier, and Varinard, p. 479; Jean-Pierre Royer, *La Société judiciaire depuis le XVIIIe siècle* (Paris: P. U. F., 1979), pp. 336–38.

27. Foyer, p. 27.

28. Martaguet, p. 113.

29. Jean Libmann, "*La 'Politisation' des juges: une vieille histoire?*" 16 *Pouvoirs* (1981), p. 52.

30. Vincent, Montagnier, and Varinard, pp. 506–8.

31. This college also proposes the members of the Prosecution Department to compose the disciplinary commission.

32. Bloch, pp. 101–5.

33. Vincent, Montagnier, and Varinard, p. 510.

34. Ibid., pp. 514–15.

35. Bodiguel, pp. 31–42; Vincent, Montagnier, and Varinard, pp. 478, 480.

36. Some women even occupy important positions. The first president of the *Cour de Cassation* is a woman.

37. Interviews of Mr. André Giresse, one by Jean-Pierre Cormerais, "*Il faut rendre la liberté à la justice*," *le Figaro-Magazine* (November 23, 1985), pp. 110–12; the other by Pierre-Etienne Pages, "*Magistrature debout*," *Valeurs Actuelles* (December 9, 1985), p. 26.

38. Kathleen Barber, "Ohio Judicial Elections—Nonpartisan Premises with Partisan Results," 32 *Ohio State Law Journal* (1971), p. 762.

39. *Book of the States, 1984–1985* (Lexington, Ky.: Council of State Governments, 1984), pp. 154–55.

40. Lawrence Baum, *American Courts: Process and Policy* (Boston: Houghton-Mifflin Co., 1986), p. 102.

41. Larry C. Berkson, "Selection of State Judges: Election or Appointment," in *Managing the State Courts: Text and Readings*, eds. Larry C. Berkson, Steven W. Hays, and Susan J. Carbon (St. Paul: West Publishing Co., 1977), p. 137.

42. Ibid.

43. Baum, p. 102.

44. Alan Neff, *The United States District Court Nominating Commissions* (Chicago: American Judicature Society, 1981).

45. W. Gary Fowler, "Judicial Selection under Reagan and Carter: A Comparison of Their Initial Recommendation Procedures," 67 *Judicature* (1984), p. 265; Elliot E. Slotnick, "The ABA Standing Committee on Federal Judiciary," 66 *Judicature* (1983), p. 348.

46. Sheldon Goldman, "Reaganizing the Judiciary," in *Courts, Judges and Politics*, eds. Walter F. Murphy and C. Herman Pritchett (New York: Random House, 1986), pp. 165–67.

47. Susan J. Carbon, "Retention Elections in the United States," 64 *Judicature* (1980), p. 213.

48. Mary L. Volcansek, "The Effects of Judicial Selection Reform: What We Know and What We Do Not," in *The Analysis of Judicial Reform*, ed. Philip L. Dubois (Lexington, Mass.: Lexington Books, 1982), p. 86.

49. Allan Ashman and James J. Alfini, *Judicial Nominating Commissions: The Key to Judicial Merit Selection* (Chicago: American Judicature Society, 1974).

50. Carbon, p. 213.

51. Baum, p. 100.

52. Philip L. Dubois, *From Ballot to Bench: Judicial Elections and the Quest for Accountability* (Austin: University of Texas Press, 1980), pp. 29–32.

53. Charles A. Johnson, Roger C. Schaefer, and R. Neal McKnight, "The Salience of Judicial Candidates and Elections," 59 *Social Science Quarterly* (1978), p. 371.

54. Philip L. Dubois, "The Significance of Voter Cues in State Supreme Court Elections," 13 *Law and Society Review* (1979), p. 757.

55. Philip L. Dubois, "Voting Cues in Nonpartisan Trial Court Elections: A Multivariate Assessment," 18 *Law and Society Review* (1984), p. 419.

56. Mary L. Volcansek, "An Exploration of the Judicial Election Process," 34 *Western Political Quarterly* (1981), p. 572.

57. Lawrence Baum, "The Electoral Fates of Incumbent Judges in the Ohio Court of Common Pleas," 66 *Judicature* (1983), p. 420.

58. Volcansek, "An Exploration," p. 572.

59. Baum, *American Courts*, p. 105.

60. Burton M. Atkins and Henry R. Glick, "Formal Judicial Recruitment and State Supreme Court Decisions," 2 *American Politics Quarterly* (1974), p. 427; Stuart S. Nagel, *Comparing Elected and Appointed Judicial Systems* (Beverly Hills, Calif.: Sage Publications, 1973).

61. John Paul Ryan, Allan Ashman, Bruce D. Sales, and Sandra Shane-DuBow, *American Trial Judges* (New York: The Free Press, 1980), pp. 126–28.

62. Mary L. Volcansek, "Why Lawyers Become Judges," 62 *Judicature* (1978), p. 175.

63. Harold J. Berman, *Law and Revolution* (Cambridge, Mass.: Harvard University Press, 1983), p. 478.

64. P. D. Dagtoglou, "The English Judges and European Community Law," 37 *Cambridge Law Journal* (1978), pp. 76–77.

65. Max Rheinstein, ed., *Max Weber on Law in Economy and Society* (Cambridge, Mass.: Harvard University Press, 1966), pp. 304–5.

66. Berman, p. 557.

67. Ibid.

68. Lester G. Seligman, Michael R. King, Chong Lim Kim, and Roland E. Smith, *Patterns of Recruitment* (Chicago: Rand McNally, 1974), p. 14.

69. Ibid., p. 15.

70. John R. Schmidhauser, "Justices of the Supreme Court: A Collective Portrait," 3 *Midwest Journal of Political Science* (February 1959), pp. 6–13.

71. Kermit L. Hall, "Social Backgrounds and Judicial Recruitment: A Nineteenth-Century Perspective on the Lower Federal Judiciary," 29 *Western Political Quarterly* (June 1976), pp. 246–51.

72. Ryan, Ashman, Sales, and Shane-DuBow, pp. 126–28.

73. Walter F. Murphy and Joseph Tanenhaus, *The Study of Public Law* (New York: Random House, 1972), p. 92.

74. Ehrmann, p. 177.

75. Donald L. Horowitz, *The Courts and Social Policy* (Washington, D. C.: The Brookings Institution, 1977), p. 3.

76. Ibid., p. 12.

77. Daniel J. Elazar, *American Federalism: A View from the States* (New York: Harper & Row, 1984), p. 110.

78. Dubois, *Ballot to Bench*, p. 43.

79. Charles H. Sheldon, *The American Judicial Process* (New York: Dodd, Mead, & Co., 1974), p. 78.

80. Baum, *American Courts*, p. 105.

81. Ehrmann, p. 179.

82. The eleventh federal judge was impeached in 1986 and convicted. Henry J. Abraham, *The Judicial Process* (Oxford: Oxford University Press, 1986), p. 45.

83. Eric Neisser, "The New Federal Judicial Discipline Act," 65 *Judicature* (1981), p. 142; Stephen B. Burbank, "The Federal Judicial Discipline Act," 67 *Judicature* (1983), p. 183; "Close Questions About Judicial Disability and Misconduct," 69 *Judicature* (1985), p. 103.

84. Joseph C. Goulden, *The Benchwarmers* (New York: Ballantine Books, 1974); William Thomas Braithwaite, *Who Judges the Judges* (Chicago: American Bar Foundation, 1971); Mary L. Volcansek, "Codes of Judicial Ethics," 17 *American Business Law Journal* (1980), p. 493.

85. Mattei Dogan and Dominique Pelassy, *How to Compare Nations: Strategies in Comparative Politics* (Chatham, N. J.: Chatham House Publishers, 1984), p. 58.

86. Wison, p. 77.

References

BOOKS

Abraham, Henry J. *The Judicial Process*. New York: Oxford University Press, 1986.

Adams, John. *The Political Writings of John Adams*. Ed. George A. Peek, Jr. New York: Liberal Arts Press, 1954.

Almond, Gabriel A., and Sidney Verba. *The Civic Culture: Political Attitudes and Democracy in Five Nations*. Princeton, N. J.: Princeton University Press, 1963.

———. *The Civic Culture Revisited*. Boston: Little, Brown & Co., 1980.

Ashman, Allan, and James J. Alfini. *Judicial Nominating Commissions: The Key to Judicial Merit Selection*. Chicago: American Judicature Society, 1974.

Aubin, Raoul. *L'Organisation judiciaire d'après les Cahiers de 1789*. Paris: Jouve, 1928.

Barrué, Jean Michel. *Voltaire et le droit pénal*. Paris, 1966.

Bassett, John Spencer. *The Federalist System, 1789–1801*. New York: Harper Brothers, 1906.

Baum, Lawrence. *American Courts: Process and Policy*. Boston: Houghton-Mifflin Co., 1986.

Beard, Charles A. *An Economic Interpretation of the Constitution of the United States*. New York: The Free Press, 1935.

———. *Economic Origins of Jeffersonian Democracy*. New York: The Free Press, 1915.

Becker, Theodore L. *Comparative Judicial Politics*. Chicago: Rand McNally, 1973.

Ben, Perley Poore. *The Federal and State Constitutions, Colonial Chart-*

ers, and Other Organic Laws of the United States, 2 vols. New York: Burt Franklin, 1877.

Berkson, Larry, Scott Beller, and Michele Grimaldi. *Judicial Selection in the United States: A Compendium of Provisions*. Chicago: American Judicature Society, 1981.

Berman, Harold J. *Law and Revolution*. Cambridge, Mass.: Harvard University Press, 1983.

Blau, Joseph L., ed. *Social Theories of Jacksonian Democracy*. New York: Liberal Arts Press, 1947.

Bluche, François. *Les Magistrats du Parlement de Paris au XVIIIe siècle (1715–1776)*. Paris: Les Belles Lettres, 1960.

Book of the States, 1984–1985. Lexington, Ky.: Council of State Governments, 1984.

Braithwaite, William Thomas. *Who Judges the Judges*. Chicago: American Bar Foundation, 1971.

Burke, Edmund. *Reflections on the Revolution in France*. Ed. Thomas H. D. Mahoney. New York: Liberal Arts Press, 1955.

Carpenter, William S. *Judicial Tenure in the United States*. New Haven, Conn.: Yale University Press, 1918.

Charle, Christophe. *Les Hauts fonctionnaires en France au XIXe siècle*. Paris: Gallimard-Julliard, 1980.

Dawson, John P. *A History of Lay Judges*. Cambridge, Mass.: Harvard University Press, 1960.

Dealey, James Q. *The Growth of American State Constitutions*. New York: Da Capo Press, 1972.

de Tocqueville, Alexis. *Democracy in America*. Ed. Phillips Bradley. New York: Vintage Books, 1954.

Dogan, Mattei, and Dominique Pelassy. *How to Compare Nations: Strategies in Comparative Politics*. Chatham, N. J.: Chatham House Publishers, 1984.

Dubois, Philip L. *From Bench to Ballot: Judicial Elections and the Quest for Accountability*. Austin: University of Texas Press, 1980.

Duguit, L., H. Monnier, and R. Bonnard. *Constitutions et principales lois politiques de la France*. 7th ed. Paris: L. G. D. J., 1952.

Ehrmann, Henry W. *Comparative Legal Cultures*. Englewood Cliffs, N. J.: Prentice-Hall, 1976.

———. *Politics in France*. Boston: Little, Brown & Co., 1982.

Elazar, Daniel J. *American Federalism: A View from the States*. New York: Harper & Row, 1984.

Ellis, Richard E. *The Jeffersonian Crisis: Courts and Politics in the Young Republic*. New York: Oxford University Press, 1971.

Ethridge, George H. *Mississippi Constitutions*. Jackson, Miss.: Tucker Printing House, 1928.

Farrand, Max. *The Framing of the Constitution of the United States*. New Haven, Conn.: Yale University Press, 1913.

Foner, Philip S., ed. *The Life and Major Writings of Thomas Paine*. Secaucus, N. J.: Citadel Press, 1948.

Ford, Paul Leicester. *Pamphlets on the Constitution of the United States*. New York: Da Capo Press, 1968.

Friedman, Lawrence M. *A History of American Law*. New York: Simon & Schuster, 1973.

Gawalt, Gerard W. *The Promise of Power: The Emergence of the Legal Profession in Massachusetts, 1760–1840*. Westport, Conn.: Greenwood Press, 1979.

Godechot, Jacques. *Les Institutions de la France sous la Révolution et l'Empire*. Paris: P. U. F., 1985.

Goulden, Joseph C. *The Benchwarmers*. New York: Ballantine Books, 1974.

Halevy, Elie. *The Growth of Philosophic Radicalism*. Boston: Beacon Press, 1966.

Hall, Kermit. *A Comprehensive Bibliography of American Constitutional and Legal History, 1896–1979*. Millwood, N. Y.: Kraus International Publications, 1984.

Hamilton, Alexander, John Jay, and James Madison. *The Federalist*. New York: The Modern Library.

Haynes, Evan. *The Selection and Tenure of Judges*. Littleton, Colo.: Fred B. Rothman & Co., 1944.

Henderson, Dwight F. *Courts for a New Nation*. Washington, D. C.: Public Affairs Press, 1971.

Horowitz, Donald L. *The Courts and Social Policy*. Washington, D. C.: The Brookings Institution, 1977.

Howard, A. E. Dick. *Commentaries on the Constitution of Virginia*. Charlottesville: University of Virginia Press, 1974.

Jefferson, Thomas. *On Democracy*. Ed. Saul K. Padover. New York: Mentor Books, 1939.

———. *The Political Writings of Thomas Jefferson*. Ed. Edward Dumbault. New York: Liberal Arts Press, 1955.

Kenyon, Cecelia M., ed. *The Antifederalists*. Indianapolis: Bobbs-Merrill Co., 1966.

Lafon, Jacqueline L. *Recherches sur la fin des juridictions d'Ancien Régime pendant la Révolution: Le Châtelet et le Parlement de Paris*. Paris, 1972.

———. *Juges et consuls. A la recherche d'un statut dans la France d'Ancien Régime*. Paris: Economica, 1981.

Limann, Hilla. *Le Contrat social de Jean-Jacques Rousseau et son influence sur les constitutions de 1791 et 1793.* Paris, 1965.

Machelon, Jean-Pierre. *La République contre les libertés?* Paris: Presses de la Fondation Nationale des Sciences Politiques, 1976.

McDonald, William. *Jacksonian Democracy, 1829–1837.* New York: Harper & Brothers, 1906.

McLaughlin, Andrew Cunningham. *The Confederation and the Constitution: 1783–1789.* New York: Harper & Brothers, 1905.

Mille, Pierre. *Voltaire et les institutions.* Reims, 1979.

Montesquieu, Baron de. *The Spirit of the Laws.* Trans. Thomas Nugent. New York: Hafner Publishing Co., 1949.

Mousnier, Roland. *Les Institutions de la France sous la monarchie absolue.* Paris: P. U. F., 1980.

Murphy, Walter F., and Joseph Tanenhaus. *The Study of Public Law.* New York: Random House, 1972.

Nader, Laura, ed. *Law in Culture and Society.* Chicago: Aldine Publishing Co., 1969.

Nagel, Stuart S. *Comparing Elected and Appointed Judicial Systems.* Beverly Hills, Calif.: Sage Publications, 1973.

Neff, Alan. *The United States District Court Nominating Commissions.* Chicago: American Judicature Society, 1981.

Nelson, William E. *Dispute and Conflict Resolution in Plymouth County, Massachusetts, 1725–1825.* Chapel Hill: University of North Carolina Press, 1981.

Olivier-Martin, François. *Histoire du Droit Français des origines à la Révolution.* Paris: Domat-Montchrestien, 1948.

Parrington, Vernon Louis. *Main Currents in American Thought.* 2 vols. New York: Harcourt, Brace, & World, 1927, 1930.

Peterson, Merrill D., ed. *The Portable Thomas Jefferson.* Harmondsworth: Penguin Press, 1977.

Prescott, Arthur Taylor. *Drafting the Federal Constitution.* Westport, Conn.: Greenwood Press, 1968.

Remini, Robert V. *The Revolutionary Age of Andrew Jackson.* New York: Harper & Row, 1976.

Rheinstein, Max, ed. *Max Weber on Law in Economy and Society.* Cambridge, Mass.: Harvard University Press, 1966.

Rossiter, Clinton. *1787: The Grand Convention.* New York: Macmillan Co., 1966.

Rousselet, Marcel. *La Magistrature sous la Monarchie de Juillet.* Paris: Sirey, 1937.

———. *Histoire de la magistrature française des origines à nos jours.* (2 vol.) Paris: Plon, 1957.

Royer, Jean-Pierre. *La Société judiciaire depuis le XVIIIe siècle*. Paris: P. U. F., 1979.

Royer, Jean-Pierre, Renée Martinage, and Pierre Lecocq. *Juges et notables au XIXe siècle*. Paris: P. U. F., 1982.

Ryan, John Paul, Allan Ashman, Bruce D. Sales, and Sandra Shane-DuBow. *American Trial Judges*. New York: The Free Press, 1980.

Sabine, George H. *A History of Political Theory*. New York: Holt, Rinehart & Winston, 1961.

Sautel, Gérard. *Histoire des Institutions Publiques depuis la Révolution Française*. Paris: Dalloz, 1974.

Schönfeld, Karel Menzo. *Montesquieu: "en la bouche . . . de la loi."* Leiden: New Rhine Publishers, 1979.

Schubert, Glendon, and David J. Danelski, *Comparative Judicial Behavior*. New York: Oxford University Press, 1969.

Seligman, Lester G., Michael R. King, Chong Lim Kim, and Roland E. Smith. *Patterns of Recruitment*. Chicago: Rand McNally, 1974.

Sheldon, Charles H. *The American Judicial Process*. New York: Dodd, Mead & Co., 1974.

Smith, Page. *The Constitution: A Documentary and Narrative History*. New York: William Morrow & Co., 1978.

Storing, Herbert J., ed. *The Anti-Federalist*. Chicago: University of Chicago Press, 1985.

Tachau, Mary K. Bonsteel. *Federal Courts in the Early Republic: Kentucky, 1789–1816*. Princeton, N. J.: Princeton University Press, 1978.

Tudesq, A. J. *Les Grands notables en France (1840–1849)*. Paris: P. U. F., 1964.

Turner, Frederick Jackson. *Rise of the New West, 1819–1829*. New York: Harper & Brothers, 1906.

Villard, Pierre. *Les Justices seigneuriales dans la Marche*. Paris: L. G. D. J., 1969.

Villers, Robert. *L'Organisation du Parlement de Paris et des conseils supérieurs d'après la réforme de Maupeou, 1771–1774*. Paris: Jouve, 1937.

Vincent, Jean, Gabriel Montagnier, and André Varinard. *La Justice et ses institutions*. Paris: Dalloz, 1982.

Warren, Charles. *The Supreme Court in United States History, 1789–1918*. Boston: Little, Brown, & Co., 1926.

Wilson, James Q. *American Government: Institutions and Politics*. Lexington, Mass.: D. C. Heath & Co. 1986.

Wood, Gordon S. *The Creation of the American Republic, 1776–1787*. Chapel Hill: University of North Carolina Press, 1969.

ARTICLES

Atkins, Burton M., and Henry R. Glick, "Formal Judicial Recruitment and State Supreme Court Decisions," 2 *American Politics Quarterly* (1974), p. 427.

Aulard, A., "The French Revolution and Napoleon," in *Modern France*. Ed. Arthur Tilley. New York: Russell & Russell, 1967.

Banks, Margaret A., "Attitudes in the Philadelphia Convention Towards the British System of Government," *American Journal of Legal History* (January 1966), pp. 15–33.

Barber, Kathleen, "Ohio Judicial Elections—Nonpartisan Premises with Partisan Results," 32 *Ohio State Law Journal* (1971), p. 762.

Baum, Lawrence, "The Electoral Fates of Incumbent Judges in the Ohio Court of Common Pleas," 66 *Judicature* (1983), p. 420.

Berkson, Larry C., "Selection of State Judges: Election or Appointment," in *Managing the State Courts: Text and Readings*. Eds. Larry C. Berkson, Steven W. Hays, and Susan J. Carbon. St. Paul: West Publishing Co., 1977, p. 131.

Bloch, Etienne, "*Faire carrière sous la Ve*," 16 *Pouvoirs, revue française d'études constitutionnelles et politiques* (1981), pp. 97–105.

Bodiguel, Jean-Luc, "*Qui sont les magistrats français? Esquisse d'une sociologie*," 16 *Pouvoirs* (1981), pp. 31–42.

Burbank, Stephen B., "The Federal Judicial Discipline Act," 67 *Judicature* (1983), p. 183.

Canon, Bradley, "The Impact of Formal Selection Processes on Characteristics of Judges—Reconsidered," 13 *Law and Society Review* (1972), p. 570.

Carbon, Susan J., "Retention Elections in the United States," 64 *Judicature* (1980), p. 213.

———. "Women in the Judiciary: An Introduction," 65 *Judicature* (1982), p. 285.

"Close Questions About Judicial Disability and Misconduct," 69 *Judicature* (1985), p. 103.

Coyle, Arlen B., "Judicial Selection and Tenure in Mississippi." 43 *Mississippi Law Journal* (1972), p. 90.

Dagtoglou, P. D., "The English Judges and European Community Law," 37 *Cambridge Law Journal* (1978), p. 75.

Dalat, Jean, "*Montesquieu, magistrat*," *Archives des lettres modernes. Les Lettres modernes*, 1971.

Danelski, David J., "The People and the Court in Japan," in *Frontiers of Judicial Research*. Eds. Joel B. Grossman and Joseph Tanenhaus. New York: John Wiley & Sons, 1969.

Desjardins, A. "*La Magistrature élue*," *La Revue des Deux Mondes*. Beauvais, 1882.

de Lapradelle, A., "Law," in *Modern France*. Ed. Arthur Tilley. New York: Russell & Russell, 1922.

Dubois, Philip L., "The Significance of Voter Cues in State Supreme Court Elections," 13 *Law and Society Review* (1979), p. 757.

———, "Voting Cues in Nonpartisan Trial Court Elections: A Multivariate Assessment," 18 *Law and Society Review* (1984), p. 419.

Dunn, Patrick Winston, "Judicial Selection in the States: A Critical Study with Proposals for Reform," 4 *Hofstra Law Review* (1976), pp. 267–353.

Foucart, "*De la nécessité d'exiger des candidats à la magistrature des conditions spéciales de capacité*," *La Revue de législation et de jurisprudence* (October 1834–March 1835), pp. 346–57.

Fowler, W. Gary, "Judicial Selection under Reagan and Carter: A Comparison of Their Initial Recommendation Procedures," 67 *Judicature* (1984), p. 265.

Foyer, Jean, "*Un Pouvoir refusé*," 16 *Pouvoirs* (1981), pp. 7–29.

Giannotti, Michèle, "*L'Agenda du magistrat, le siège*," 16 *Pouvoirs* (1981), pp. 119–26.

Goldman, Sheldon, "Backgrounds, Attitudes, and Voting Behavior of Judges," 31 *Journal of Politics* (1969), p. 214.

———. "Reaganizing the Judiciary," in *Courts, Judges and Politics*. Eds. Walter F. Murphy and C. Hermann Pritchett. New York: Random House, 1986, p. 165.

Grossman, Joel B., "Social Backgrounds and Judicial Decision-making," 79 *Harvard Law Review* (1966), p. 1551.

Grossman, Joel B., and Austin Sarat, "Political Culture and Judicial Research," 2 *Washington University Law Review* (1971), p. 192.

Hall, Kermit, "Progressive Reform and the Decline of Democratic Accountability: The Popular Election of State Supreme Court Judges, 1850–1920," *1984 American Bar Foundation Research Journal* (1984), pp. 347–48.

———, "Social Backgrounds and Judicial Recruitment: A Nineteenth-Century Perspective on the Lower Federal Judiciary," 29 *Western Political Quarterly* (June 1976), pp. 243–57.

Jacob, Herbert, "The Effect of Institutional Differences in the Recruitment Process: The Case of State Judges," 13 *Journal of Politics* (1964), p. 104.

Johnson, Charles A., Roger C. Schaefer, and R. Neal McKnight, "The Salience of Judicial Candidates and Elections," 59 *Social Science Quarterly* (1978), p. 371.

Laski, Harold J. "The Technique of Judicial Appointment," 26 *Michigan Law Review* (1926), p. 529.

Libmann, Jean, "*La 'Politisation' des juges: une vieille histoire?*" 16 *Pouvoirs* (1981), p. 43–53.

Lyon-Caen, Pierre, "*Le Syndicat de la Magistrature," 16 Pouvoirs* (1981), pp. 55–68.

Macridis, Roy C., "France," in *Modern Political Systems: Europe*. Ed. Roy C. Macridis. Englewood Cliffs: N. J.: Prentice-Hall, 1983.

Martaguet, Pierre, "*Comment devient-on magistrat?*" 16 *Pouvoirs* (1981), pp. 107–17.

Neisser, Eric, "The New Federal Judicial Discipline Act," 65 *Judicature* (1981), p. 142.

Pound, Roscoe, "The Causes of Popular Dissatisfaction with the Administration of Justice," reprinted in 20 *Journal of the American Judicature Society* (1937), p. 178.

Sarda, François, "*Le Pouvoir et les instances judiciaires*," 16 *Pouvoirs* (1981), pp. 69–78.

Schmidhauser, John R., "Justices of the Supreme Court: A Collective Portrait," 3 *Midwest Journal of Political Science* (February 1959), pp. 6–13.

Seis, Dennis E., "Selecting Judges in the States: A Brief History and Analysis," 9 *Northern Kentucky Law Review* (1982), p. 459.

Slotnick, Elliot E., "The ABA Standing Committee on Federal Judiciary," 66 *Judicature* (1983), p. 348.

———, "The Paths to the Federal Bench: Gender, Race and Judicial Recruitment," 67 *Judicature* (1984), p. 371.

Troper, Michel, "*Fonction juridictionnelle ou pouvoir judiciaire?*" 16 *Pouvoirs* (1981), pp. 5–15.

Vanderbilt, Arthur F., "Judges and Jurors: Their Functions, Qualifications and Selection," 36 *Boston University Law Review* (1956), p. 1.

Volcansek, Mary L., "Codes of Judicial Ethics," 17 *American Business Law Journal* (1980), p. 493.

———, "Conventional Wisdom of Court Reform," in *Managing the State Courts: Text and Readings*. Eds. Larry C. Berkson, Steven W. Hayes, and Susan J. Carbon. St. Paul: West Publishing Co., 1977, pp. 18–23.

———, "The Effects of Judicial Selection Reform: What We Know and What We Do Not," in *The Analysis of Judicial Reform*. Ed. Philip L. Dubois. Lexington, Mass.: Lexington Books, 1982, p. 86.

———, "An Exploration of the Judicial Election Process," 34 *Western Political Quarterly* (1981), p. 572.

———, "Why Lawyers Become Judges," 62 *Judicature* (1978), p. 175.

Winters, Glenn R., "Selection of Judges—An Historical Introduction," 44 *Texas Law Review* (1966), p. 1081.

Index

About the Authors

MARY L. VOLCANSEK is Professor of Political Science at Florida International University. She is the author of *Judicial Politics in Europe: An Impact Analysis,* and has written for *Justice Systems Journal, Judicature, Policy Studies Quarterly, Western Political Quarterly,* and *American Business Law Journal.*

JACQUELINE LUCIENNE LAFON is Associate Dean of the Faculty of Law at the University of Paris South. She is the author of *Les Deputes du Commerce et l'Ordonnance de mar 1673* and *Juges et Consuls: A la recherche d'un statut dans la France d'Ancien Régime* and has written for *Etudes d'Histoire du Droit Parisien* and *Revue historique de Droit Français et Etranger.*